GUILLERMO
DEL TORO

THE ICONIC FILMMAKER AND HIS WORK

Brimming with creative inspiration, how-to projects and useful information to enrich your everyday life, Quarto Knows is a favourite destination for those pursuing their interests and passions. Visit our site and dig deeper with our books into your area of interest: Quarto Creates, Quarto Cooks, Quarto Homes, Quarto Lives, Quarto Drives, Quarto Explores, Quarto Gifts, or Quarto Kids.

First published in 2021 by White Lion Publishing,
an imprint of The Quarto Group.
The Old Brewery, 6 Blundell Street
London, N7 9BH,
United Kingdom
T (0)20 7700 6700
www.QuartoKnows.com

Text © 2021 Ian Nathan

A catalogue record for this book is available from the British Library.

ISBN 978 0 71126 328 4
Ebook ISBN 978 0 71126 329 1

10 9 8 7 6 5 4 3 2 1

Designed by Sue Pressley and Paul Turner, Stonecastle Graphics Ltd

Printed in China

GUILLERMO
DEL TORO

THE ICONIC FILMMAKER AND HIS WORK

IAN NATHAN

UNOFFICIAL AND UNAUTHORISED

WHITE
LION
PUBLISHING

CONTENTS

INTRODUCTION

Monster, n. 1. a. Originally: a mythical creature which is part animal and part human, or combines elements of two or more animal forms, and is frequently of great size and ferocious appearance. Later, more generally: any imaginary creature that is large, ugly, and frightening. **b.** In extended and figurative use. Formerly also in collocations like *faultless monster, monster of perfection*, indicating an astonishing or unnatural degree of excellence. **2.** Something extraordinary or unnatural; an amazing event or occurrence; a prodigy, a marvel. *Obsolete*. Also: an extraordinarily large example of something.[1]

Merriam-Webster Dictionary

There are many ways to sum up the life and films of the marvellous Guillermo del Toro. But fundamentally, he is the kind of artist who can name his favourite of all Fu Manchu's cunning traps – from the original books by Sax Rohmer, naturally. Rohmer, he would add by way of context, had been a good friend of Harry Houdini. Fu Manchu, meanwhile, is the Chinese criminal mastermind with a moustache that descends to his navel like tendrils.

So, the trap: the good guys are informed that through the next door resides Fu Manchu's most fiendish device. They ready their revolvers, stir their courage and enter… an empty room. There is nothing there at all. Then suddenly a mushroom blooms from the mouth of one of the party. Then another, and another: all these mushrooms sprouting from their noses, mouths and eyes. The room has been full of spores!

'I love that,'[2] said del Toro.

You see, del Toro is Fu Manchu. He takes empty rooms and transforms them into devious traps. He does the unexpected. The Mexican-born director, with his easy manner and grand mind, his unending serial enthusiasms, is really a magician. He wants to ensnare our imaginations, with horror, fairy-tale, science fiction, gothic romance, gaudy superheroes, puppets, or film noir, and we are never ready.

The first time I met him was to discuss *Pan's Labyrinth*, perhaps the high watermark of his varied filmography. Though there are days when, like him, I see the ghosts of *The Devil's Backbone* as the emblem of his mix of fantasy and feeling. And others still when I crave nothing more than the scarlet embrace of *Hellboy*.

We sat in what his hotel called its library: hard-backed classics, oak panelling, ersatz-Victorian sconces, leather armchairs, and an antique table as polished as a magic mirror.

Right: The eyes have it - when Guillermo del Toro looks upon the world with those baby blues he sees magic.

I half-expected Sherlock Holmes or Edgar Allan Poe's Auguste Dupin to stroll in and shake his hand. It was like an outpost of Bleak House, the Los Angeles mansion he has transformed into a repository of all that inspires him: the books, films, paintings, comics, magazines, even medical journals, that nourish his storytelling. Including the complete Fu Manchu. Del Toro is explicit about the sources of his films, proud of them. He has an ongoing dialogue with the past. He stands on the shoulders of giants (and giant robots).

Asking him a question was like stepping into a waterfall.

I feared my allotted time would be used up by my first tentative enquiry. His mind is wildly discursive. He spans from the intricacies of Faun management to Hitchcock's neglected gems (FYI: *Topaz* and *Family Plot*) in a heartbeat. Thoughts tumbled over one another in their eagerness to be heard.

He seemed to be asking and answering his own questions.

Only Quentin Tarantino comes close in terms of contextualizing and mythologizing their work. It's as if every interview is another chapter in a grand, leather-bound biography.

Del Toro's approach is that of an auteur, but without pretension. Getting in ahead of the academics and critics, he deconstructs his own films: pointing out the threads that lead back to his Mexican childhood, or the desired psychological effect of a particular colour scheme, or all the allegorical furniture, which is quite often also actual furniture. How the mother's bed in *Pan's Labyrinth* comes subtly inscribed with horned motifs.

The texture of things is so important: he builds exquisite sets and props and monsters, only reverting to CGI for the impossible.

Yet del Toro is anything but dark. He is a big-hearted, passionate, even sentimental (that Latin blood!) man. He loves to laugh, is big on pranks and one-liners, and giggles at the madness of it all, especially Hollywood and its preening absurdities. Hellboy's laconic comebacks are pure del Toro.

"There is no more terrifying horror than the one that is intimate,"[3] he once said. Every film in his canon is personal, no matter how much blood is splattered on a sewer wall.

There have been projects as dear to him as children that have never made it the screen. Hollywood has often struggled to decipher the riddle he presents – artist or thrill seeker? Gore hound or poet? The answer is all of the above. The loss of his great H.P. Lovecraft epic *At the Mountains of Madness* is a wound that will never fully heal. And so be it – each lost film lives on inside him. His scars, like the battle for *Mimic*, a third *Hellboy*, or his unmade *Hobbits*, are blueprints for the next great idea.

Left: A horrified Ofelia looks on at her mother's decline in *Pan's Labyrinth*. The motif of the Faun's horns is inscribed into the frame of the bed.

Right: Del Toro stands proudly on the snowy set of *Crimson Peak* – with the great Mexican director the lavish sets say as much as the actors.

His own backstory is full of wonder. How he grew up in relative affluence in the suburbs of Guadalajara, the product of a practical father, a magical mother, and an angry grandmother. He was raised a reluctant Catholic, with all its ceremony and guilt. Being Mexican is not just his nationality, it is his superpower. All his films, wherever he made them, and with whoever's money, are Mexican films.

Del Toro had a single-mindedness and God-or-otherwise-given talent that took him first to study film at university – and he can rival Martin Scorsese in off-the-cuff cinematic knowledge. Then to the local television industry – where he began making monsters (literally). To getting his first feature off the ground in contemporary vampire fable *Cronos*. That was our first taste of an exotic cocktail that has been poured into thirteen films.

Who else mixes Freud with Stan Lee, Buñuel with Godzilla, Charlotte Brontë with Satan, Goya with Fu Manchu?

What you have in your hands is a celebration, a guide, a concordance, and a chart to the *terra incognita* of that extraordinary imagination – here be monsters, indeed. Film by film, picture by beautiful picture, it is a chance to bathe in that waterfall.

The other secret to del Toro as an artist (and don't forget that he also paints, sculpts, writes, pens heady verse, and designs videogames) is that he is deadly serious. Like the great fairy-tale scribes he adores – Hans Christian Andersen, those Brothers Grimm, and Charles Perrault – he delves for the roots of the world. What is it that makes mankind so magical? Why are the worst monsters always human?

'You don't do the movie you need,' he explained, 'you do the one that needs you.'[4]

ONCE UPON A TIME IN MEXICO

The early years & Cronos (1993)

How a strange and precocious Mexican childhood fostered a love of monsters and magic, and began a journey to becoming a filmmaker who would reinvent genre, starting with an inside-out vampire story

At the age of five, Guillermo del Toro began his Christmas list with a request for mandrake root. For the purposes of black magic, he made clear to his parents. He had hopes of transforming it into a baby, or some kind of homunculus. His mother, Guadalupe, took this in her stride, maybe even with a twinkle of pride in her dark eyes. She was, after all, a poet and devoted disciple of the Tarot. His father was confounded. Federico was a man of little imagination, del Toro recalled fondly, and his strange and marvellous career may have been based on his simple desire to trouble this sweet-natured man. His grandmother was horrified. A proud Catholic matriarch, she was fixated on her grandson's spiritual wellbeing, like a dowager Torquemada. Such was the severity of her conviction

that sin stirred beneath her grandson's pale skin, she would exorcise him twice a day with holy water, and place upturned bottle tops in his shoes in order to make his feet bleed like a stigmata. Guadalupe was required to intervene.

Many moons later, young Ofelia, the dark-eyed heroine and devotee of fairy-tale lore at the centre of *Pan's Labyrinth*, surely the finest illustration of del Toro's black magic, places a mandrake root bathed in milk beneath her ailing mother's bed. Her intention is to use the powers of the earth to heal. Discovered by her tyrannical stepfather, and tossed into the fire, the mandrake howls like a baby. It was 'a plant that dreams of being a human,'[1] foretold the Faun, Ofelia's mentor and malefactor. He should know: he appears to be as much flora as fauna.

Above left: A baby-faced Guillermo del Toro during the making of *Cronos* in 1993, eager to introduce the pleasures of genre to Mexican filmmaking.

Above: Captain Vidal (Sergi López) discovers the mandrake root hidden beneath the bed in *Pan's Labyrinth* – an image that finds its origins in del Toro's childhood fascinations.

There were already monsters lurking in Guillermo's bedroom. Splayed across the floor was this awful lime-green shagpile – like something that belonged to Austin Powers. Staring at it from his crib, he saw a sea of green fingers waiting to drag him into the depths.

'So I wet my bed, and my mother spanked me,' he recalled. 'One day, I got tired of the spanking and got up in my crib and climbed down and said to the monsters, "If you allow me to go pee, I'll be your friend forever."'[2] He has peed happily ever since.

Homage has been paid to the ancient gods of the shagpile in a profusion of mossy tentacles and giant, pea-green Elementals. In their own way, each of del Toro's screen fables is an extension of what he termed the 'lucid dreaming'[3] he had as a boy. The boy he remains.

'Guillermo has that child within himself, and that is what is amazing about him,' appreciated longtime producer Bertha Navarro. 'I think that is a very powerful and unique way of seeing things.'[4]

In other words, he is Hellboy; he is Ofelia; he is Geppetto carving a son out of wood.

Born on October 9, 1964, it will come as no surprise to discover a complicated, imaginative, if slightly unwholesome child living comfortably in a white-walled mansion in a middle-class suburb of the Mexican city of Guadalajara. A lottery win had blessed the family with an upgraded lifestyle. His father started a Chrysler dealership. His son started a menagerie: snakes, rats, and one ruminative cow. Guillermo's bedroom became a cocoon lined with books, comics and figurines of monsters. (Now a celebrated director, his lifestyle upgraded again, he has two entire houses devoted to volumes of folklore and history, leather-bound novels, dime store paperbacks, five thousand comic books, props, paintings, anatomical models, clockwork automatons, and all manner of figurines, including a life-sized statue of Boris Karloff being transformed into *Frankenstein's* forlorn creature by the great make-up artist Jack Pierce.)

Back then, Guillermo was as skinny as a broomstick, with a mop of thick white hair hanging over bright blue eyes. 'People thought I was an albino,'[5] he laughed. He was an outsider, a misfit, ignored by his peers; content with the company of his brother Federico and sister Susana, or the books that filled his shelves. Guillermo's precocious head was always burrowing into dark and fantastical stories as he ventured from Marvel comics (mainly those of a horror persuasion) and fairy tales to Lovecraft, Poe, Baudelaire, and Dickens.

Or he would be drawing pictures, as adept with architectural sketches as with copying the big-breasted female warriors in the racy comic book *Heavy Metal* that arrived by mail from the fabled land of America. To terrify the nanny, he learned how to apply fake gashes to his cherub cheeks using the skin-tightening properties of collodion. The anatomical illustrations from *The Family Health Guide and Medical Encyclopedia* on his father's shelf proved highly informative.

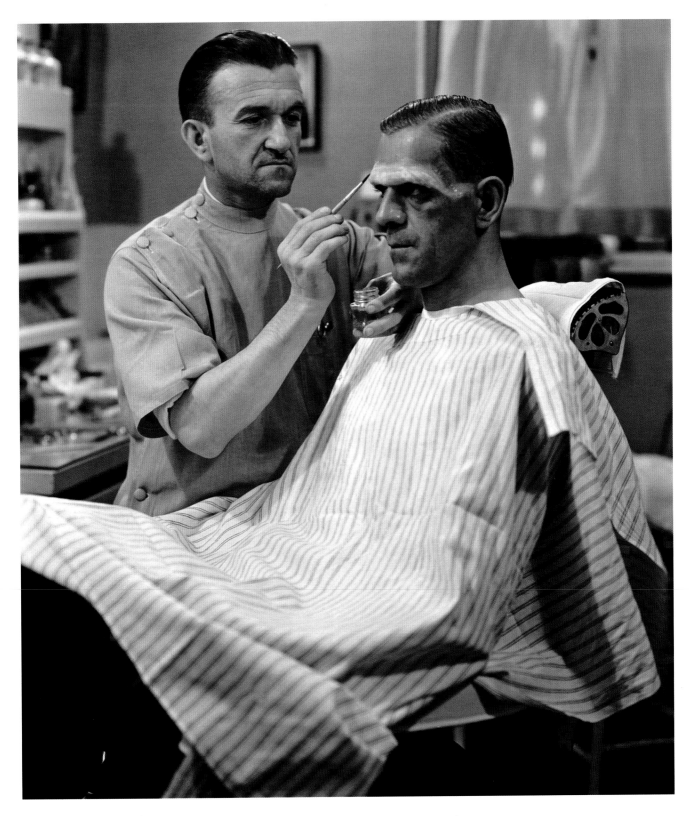

Left: Del Toro saw the 1939 version of *Wuthering Heights*, starring Laurence Olivier and Merle Oberon, while still in his mother's arms.

Opposite: Julie Adams escapes the clutches of the Gill-man in a publicity still for *Creature from the Black Lagoon* (1954), another classic monster-movie planted like a seed in Guillermo del Toro's imagination.

'My brother and I would do full human figures with clay and Plasticine – liver, intestines, the heart – fill them with ketchup and throw them from the roof,' he recalled happily. 'So I was an artistic, but very morbid kid.'[6]

His earliest memory of the cool darkness of a cinema was glimpsing scenes from the Merle Oberon-Laurence Olivier version of *Wuthering Heights* with his parents. Only an infant, he kept falling asleep and the film took on the texture of a dream. Its 'gothic spirit,'[7] he claimed, marked him for life. Soon enough he was devouring the creature features, horrors, and sci-fi on Sunday morning television, and leaping on a bus to the local fleapits to catch new releases. American movies might have held sway over impressionable

Mexican hearts, but del Toro sought out Godzilla epics and anime from Japan, martial arts films from Hong Kong, British ghost stories, and scattered offerings from Mexican filmmakers. But his Holy Trinity, he told a packed audience at Lumière Festival in Lyon, France in October 2017, 'was made up of *Frankenstein*, *The Creature from the Black Lagoon*, and werewolves.'[8]

He was the boy who loved monsters. 'When Mexico was conquered, there was a phenomenon called syncretism, in which the Catholic religion of the conquerors fused with the old religion,' he explained with a typically colourful analogy. 'In my case, that happened with Catholicism and monsters. They fused. When I was a young

kid, I truly was redeemed by these figures. Where other people saw horror, I saw beauty.'[9]

He has never fully recovered from reading Mary Shelley's *Frankenstein* when he was nine. Far from being terrified, he saw the creature as a teenage rebel escaping the grip of a tyrannical father. This fascination with what he saw as misunderstood fiends would become a life's pursuit.

As a teenager he put on weight, and has argued with his waistline ever since. But it suits him, his bearlike figure. He is a larger-than-life character, beholden to appetites of the flesh and mind. 'I'm fat because I can't contain myself,' he laughed. 'If you bring me four tortillas, I won't eat one, I'll eat all four. The same thing happens with genres.'[10]

The day he discovered the cult American magazine *Famous Monsters of Filmland* on the shelves of the local supermarket was the beginning of a beautiful friendship. He learned to speak English primarily to decipher its corny prose. Editor Forrest J. Ackerman was the patron saint of del Toro's shadowy religion. A sometime agent, author, producer, actor, magazine editor, and monster aficionado, with a hint of Vincent Price about his high forehead and pencil moustache, and a vast collection of memorabilia housed in a sweeping Los Angeles manor, which included Bela Lugosi's cape from the 1931 *Dracula*, and the monocle sported by Fritz Lang while he directed *Metropolis*.

Ackerman showed him he wasn't alone.

So baby Guillermo is now the young del Toro (which translates to 'the bull'), and not content to simply watch and read about films. When he rented Super 8 reels, absurdly abbreviated versions of B-movies like Boris Karloff's *Curse of the Crimson Altar*, the sensation of light passing through the celluloid in his father's projector whispered to him of infinite possibility. Commandeering the family's Super 8 camera, he began staging stop-motion battles between his toys – giant robots duelling gargantuan beasts.

'I took the rolls of film to the pharmacy in a kind of ecstasy,'[11] he recalled. To this day, with millions of dollars at his disposal, he still seeks that same sharp pleasure.

He soon became more ambitious. At high school, he made a short about a monster that crawled out of the toilet. Two early experiments in 16mm and 35mm featured his glamorous mother in the lead. Del Toro embraces any Freudian readings of a zombie tearing her eye out and biting into her neck in

1987's *Geometria*. 'Before that she acted in an even more bizarre short called *Matilde*,' he said with undisguised glee. 'It was about a woman who has a psychosexual obsession with a crack in the wall of her bedroom, out of which emerges a gigantic blind foetus which strangles her.'[12]

Surreal, David Lynch-like obsessions continue to course beneath the surface of his films. Sexual interpretations of his imagery being met with a delighted cry of, 'Of course, I'm a pervert!'[13]

We shouldn't mistake del Toro for simply a geek made good, content to hide in the thickets of genre. At

Above: Horror superstar Vincent Price and *Famous Monsters of Filmland* founder Forrest J. Ackerman peruse some pertinent issues. Both in their own ways are heroes for Guillermo del Toro.

Opposite: Witch-themed shocker *Curse of the Crimson Altar* was one of the B-movies del Toro rented on Super-8 reels, thrilling to the chance to project films in his own home.

film school, the newly inaugurated Centro de Investigación y Estudios Cinematográficos, a faculty he helped establish on the campus of the University of Guadalajara, he immersed himself in the breadth of the medium. His entry in the university yearbook for 1982 – beside a picture of del Toro sporting a villainous ensemble of tuxedo and shades – described him as a 'cinephile at heart'[14] who 'impelled'[15] his friends to come with him to the movie theatre.

Like his demonstrative contemporary Quentin Tarantino, del Toro readily anoints the wide range of directors from whom he draws inspiration. Interviews will be happily diverted into discussions of Akira Kurosawa, Stanley Kubrick, David Lean, Ingmar Bergman, or Steven Spielberg. Then, without taking a breath, he'll swerve into a deconstruction of the extravagant whimsy of Terry Gilliam, the lurid colour schemes of Dario Argento, or the symbolism of Chilean maestro Alejandro Jodorowsky.

Aged only 23, del Toro published a book on Alfred Hitchcock running to 546 pages. On the cover, which he designed, he portrayed himself as a bird perched on the great director's cigar. Hitchcock presides over his sensibility like a god.

'I take his word as gospel,' he said, 'but I don't think I ever tried to imitate anything he did. I try to use his words as advice, and his introspection and his wisdom as a guide.'[16] They shared a likeness: Hitchcock was a big man, a lapsed Catholic, and a skilled draftsman, who devised his films as if they were blueprints for complex and deadly traps.

Listening to del Toro talk, you realize that taking a different doorway in life could have made him a fine film critic. In fact, for a decade he wrote about film for a small Mexican newspaper, as well as doing stints on local television and radio. 'I was the one doing interpretations of *other* people's movies,'[17] he laughed. Del Toro is a rare director who willingly discusses the work of his contemporaries.

Del Toro's other filmmaking god is Luis Buñuel. The great Spanish surrealist had his similarities to Hitchcock. Both lived bourgeois, middle-class lives. 'But in their imaginations they were anarchists,'[18] relished del Toro. They were both, he said, 'interested in cruelty in the same obsessive Catholic way.'[19]

Yet stylistically they were polar opposites. Buñuel, who revived a dormant career in Mexico, trusted to his subconscious, the magic of happenstance or destiny. His films rarely felt the need to explain themselves. Like del Toro, he had large, searching eyes and a devil's smile.

Asked why he was so often drawn to the realms of film noir and the fantastic, del Toro replied that it was because they weren't considered respectable genres. All art is disobedience, he told an audience of fellow directors. You have to disobey your family. You have to disobey your teachers at film school. You have to disobey convention.

Accordingly, he sees little use for the class distinctions of high and low culture. Del Toro is as drawn to the comic-book cells of Jack Kirby as to the paintings of Goya, Picasso, Degas, Manet and Klee, which he first sampled in the ten volumes of *How to Look at Art* his father had obtained to raise the cultural outlook of the household. 'I transit between these parameters in absolute freedom,'[20] he said, and with absolute passion and sincerity. Everything he consumes – the books, comics, films, television shows, magazines, artworks, music, and video games – serves as pieces of mosaic in his films.

Life too would play its part. Growing up in Mexico, even in a quiet suburb, you were never far from violence. How many directors who so readily portray bloodshed can claim to have seen real bodies, real death, or taken their share of punches and worse?

'I have a scar from a stabbing on my leg,' admitted del Toro. 'I've been in fierce fucking fistfights. I'm not a wilting fucking flower.'[21] This isn't some macho boast; it's the exact opposite. He knows, first hand, that

Above: The other vital influence on del Toro was Alfred Hitchcock, Hollywood's master of suspense, who helped forge the medium with such radiant greats as *Rear Window*.

there is no one lonelier than the person who hates.

There is a story he tells. A fable, almost, that takes unexpected turns. As a youth on the streets of Guadalajara, he saw a man stumbling toward him, his skull split open and blood pouring down his face. He clearly wasn't mentally stable, but del Toro managed to steer him to the nearest hospital. The next day he returned to see how he was, only to find he had escaped from the mental ward. 'What kind of hospital is this?'[22] he demanded. That is how he ended up volunteering. And that is how he got to know the embalmers in the morgue. Which is where he saw a pile of foetuses.

He can pinpoint this as the moment his faith lapsed. Good or evil, he concluded, we all end up as rotten garbage. You never truly leave the church. It's always there, in the blood, and in all the crumbling chapels and holy effigies of his films. It's just that he has become estranged. 'I believe in two things,' he once wrote: 'God and time. Both are infinite, both reign supreme. Both crush mankind.'[23]

Before his childhood was over he had seen the decapitated body of a boy on a barbwire fence, and the corpse of driver inside a burning VW Beetle. 'I've seen people being shot,' he said, not nonchalantly, but unfazed. 'I've had guns put to my head… because Mexico is still a very violent place.'[24]

For all their otherworldly splendour and humour, del Toro's films are the stories of a man who has seen anguish in close-up. Blood will flow. Children will perish. Unbridled violence and beauty go hand in hand. 'Death is the ultimate goal of life,' he preached. 'I am Mexican and will never cease to be Mexican.'[25]

As biographer and friend Marc Scott Zicree so eloquently says, 'his heart of darkness is authentic.'[26]

In the early eighties, while still at film school, del Toro conceived of the story with which he would make his debut as director. It was to be a revolutionary take on the vampire movie – a subgenre in which he was, naturally, well versed, and knew to be a mythology congealed with clichés. So he was going to make a vampire film where the word 'vampire' was never uttered.

The most important movies of your life, claimed del Toro with the conviction of a mountaintop sage, are the first one and the latest one. The first one, he explained, 'articulates your universe.'[27]

Cronos contains the essence of the anticlockwise thinking with which he would approach his entire career. The hidebound conventions of genre were going to be overturned. 'I take the central monster figure and make it the saddest figure in the tale,' he said. 'The saddest vampire ever made.'[28]

It was also be the first of many films to take root in the border country between horror and fairy tale.

At heart, said del Toro, this was 'an autobiography'[29] of his tempestuous relationship with his grandmother. But one, he insisted, that was 'full of love.'[30] He would simply invert the genders. *Cronos* tells of a small girl's unconditional love for her grandfather, an antique dealer who comes by an ancient gold-plated medallion shaped like an Egyptian scarab.

This strange prize is concealed within a wooden carving of an archangel, the first of many secrets in del Toro's films that lie hidden within statues like a Russian doll (stories concealed in stories). This particular windup objet d'art has unforeseen properties, gouging its needle-like stinger into the old man's palm and feeding on him like a leech in an occult fusion of technology, biology, and the supernatural. Indeed, like stigmata.

Above: An early poster design for *Cronos*, Guillermo del Toro's remarkable inversion of the vampire formula, which incorporates his own pen-and-ink sketches.

Opposite: Aurora (Tamara Shanath) and her grandfather Jesús Gris (Federico Luppi) examine their discovery – the fateful Cronos Device.

This is the Cronos Device, said to impart eternal life (or a living death). Somewhere inside is an immortal insect. The biomechanical apparitions of H.R. Giger were not so far away. Neither was Kafka. Gradually, the grandfather will metamorphose into what is clearly a vampire – the craving for blood is a dead giveaway.

Along with early versions of his ghost story, *The Devil's Backbone*, then set in the Mexican Revolution of 1910, del Toro would work on the script every day for eight years under the more obvious provisional title of *Vampire of the Grey Dawn*. Drafts came and went, as he developed key themes

of addiction, family, and man's quest for immortality, known historically as alchemy. He began to set down ideas in beautiful, annotated ink-based drawings, embedding references within the fabric of the story.

The revised title hearkened back to Greek mythology. Cronos was the Titan who devoured his children, consuming all their years like a vampire. He would become a personification of time.

The classic European concept of the vampire would be invested with a distinctive Mexican blend of Catholic and pagan, those squabbling gods that will preside over all his films. The

symbolic consumption of the flesh and blood of Christ in consecrated bread and wine at Mass was, as he saw it, a form of vampirism. He defined *Cronos* as a 'pagan reinterpretation of the Gospel.'[31] Hence his elderly vampire's name, Jesús Gris: resurrected on the third day.

Conscious of budget constraints, it would have to be a contemporary story, set in Veracruz. Del Toro didn't know it yet, but this was to be the only film he would ever make on home soil. Nevertheless, his Mexican tale would be imbued with the classicism of those early 1930s Universal horrors and the lush, almost vulgar colours of Terence

Fisher's Hammer Horror pictures. 'His framing was impeccable,'[32] cooed del Toro, and the scene where light perforates the roof to burn Jesús Gris's skin is a direct lift from *Dracula A.D. 1972*, which starred Christopher Lee. Del Toro was also determined to open events with the gusto of an American movie: a 'grand gesture'[33] before settling down into his family melodrama.

It is the perfect entrance into the world of Guillermo del Toro – announced by a conspicuous ticking of clocks, before a resonant voice-over takes charge (Mexican TV star Jorge Martínez de Hoyos). The year is 1536,

and across what will become one of his favourite devices – the introductory montage – we meet an alchemist in his sprawling mansion cluttered with antiquities, and discover that he is the creator of the Cronos Device. As the Inquisition encroaches, he conceals his MacGuffin inside a statue. Cut to 400 years later, 1937, when a perfectly preserved body will be discovered in the ruins of a collapsed house, with marble-white skin, and its heart pierced by a stake.

Sit down with del Toro for an interview, and the answers come in torrents: references, jokes, trade secrets, and bountiful anecdotes. It's enough

Opposite: The vampire blues – Federico Luppi as Jesús Gris discovers that immortality is not what it's cracked up to be in *Cronos*. His striking corpse-like pallor had been born out of Guillermo del Toro's background in make-up effects.

Below: The poster for *Dracula A.D. 1972*, starring Christopher Lee as the legendary vampire, which provided visual inspiration for the games that del Toro played with the genre.

to make your head spin. But as a small boy he was effectively mute. He lived in his head, as silent as the grave, but in photos of him at that age there is an air of secret amusement. He would make Aurora, the tiny heroine of *Cronos*, equally mute and equally self-possessed as she calmly monitors her grandfather's decline.

'She's not innocent,' he said, 'she's *pure*.'[34] She's unable to distinguish between the living and the dead.

In truth, the girl's affection for her *'abuelo'* is only deepened by the situation. Their roles are reversed. Child becomes adult. Adult becomes Dracula. Like a dainty Renfield, Aurora puts Jesús Gris to sleep in a toy box rather than a coffin. The creature, explained del Toro, was a 'monster

being monstrous, but not being feared but loved and cared for.'[35]

Years from now, del Toro would walk away with an armful of Oscars for his tale of a mute janitor who falls in love with a sea creature in *The Shape of Water*. In these, his smaller, more allegorical films, there is a drift toward the purity of silent cinema. 'A perfect film has no dialogue,'[36] he has said. The sublime solemnity of Buster Keaton and Charlie Chaplin form another tributary of influence.

Del Toro felt no dread of working with children. A child's perspective is vital to his films: consider the orphaned boys of *The Devil's Backbone*, and stray Ofelia in *Pan's Labyrinth*: even Hellboy is a juvenile superhero (the clue is in the name). The director

has an instinct for drawing out mature performances from his young stars. Treating them like adults. 'You have to find a child who has something of the character within themselves,'[37] he said, and Tamara Shanath radiates a wordless serenity.

Beneath his corpse-like pallor, Jesús Gris clings to his humanity, straining not to succumb to his ghastly pangs for human blood. 'The power of choice,' proclaimed del Toro, 'is the essence of the human soul.'[38] Few films have shown us the grotesque struggle in being a vampire like this. What Kenneth Turan of the *Los Angeles Times* called the 'wear and tear of vampiredom.'[39]

In counterpart, we have the actual villains, who are near enough human. A soulless millionaire named de la Guardia, sealed in an antiseptic chamber like a cold flash of sci-fi across the dusky film, seeks to stall the cancer consuming his body by getting his hands on the Cronos Device. He will dispatch his quirky, bull-like nephew, Angel (an American, as it turns out) to punch his way wearily to the prize.

So del Toro's storytelling began its elegant tightrope walk of contradictions: heart and horror, fantasy and reality, whimsy and violence, originality and quotation, art and commerce. It is a blend of opposites like the peppery sweetness of Mexican food.

On a more practical footing, with *Cronos*, he was also determined to prove that Mexican cinema could create make-up effects to rival Hollywood. But nowhere in Mexico was remotely capable of the parchment pale, skin-peeling decomposition planned for Jesús Gris. So he would simply have to start his own make-up firm. Beyond his immediate ambitions for *Cronos*, this made practical sense. Make-up effects offered an immediate angle into the business, and a potential revenue stream. The company, Necropia, would eventually be founded in 1985.

In order to raise his homegrown talent to a Hollywood standard, del Toro had the chutzpah to send a letter to make-up wizard Dick Smith, in which he proposed to come to New York to serve as the great man's apprentice. Like many young cineastes, del Toro idolised Smith's (sometimes literally) revolutionary grotesques in *The Exorcist*, *Scanners* and *The Hunger*. He made the supernatural tangible. Remarkably, Smith was so taken with this audacious entreaty from Mexico that he accepted de Toro as a student. A young J.J. Abrams was

a fellow classmate – not that there was a classroom. The pair were put straight into Smith's workshop, where they had to show their talents with glue and gore, mastering authentic prosthetics.

'I think that without Dick Smith I wouldn't be a filmmaker,' said del Toro, 'he was instrumental in making the tools available to me that I needed to make *Cronos*.'[40]

That, though, would still have to wait until 1993. Returning from New York, he was diverted into television. *La Hora Marcada* (which roughly translates as 'The Appointed Time') was a Mexican take on *The Twilight Zone*, each week providing a new tale of the uncanny pierced with black humour. These made good use of Necropia's range of monsters and props, but more importantly gave del Toro his first shot as writer and director. *The Gourmets*, made in 1986, one of five microcosms of del Toro at his most devilish, features a restaurant that serves human flesh. It was during his tenure on *La Hora Marcada* that he

first collaborated with fellow director Alfonso Cuarón.

They didn't know it yet, but del Toro, Cuarón, and contemporary Alejandro González Iñárritu would form the vanguard of a new wave of dynamic Mexican directors, pioneering an intriguing balance between Hollywood production values and Mexican passion. Within fifteen years, each was to win a Best Director Oscar.

More immediately, del Toro fell in with producer Bertha Navarro and her brother, the gruff but talented cinematographer Guillermo Navarro, who had been persuaded by the unexpected quality of the screenplay to help him make *Cronos*. 'I thought, "Wow! This guy is so young, but so mature,"[41] recalled Bertha Navarro. Nonetheless, it would take her another year to raise the money. Even at a conservative $1.5 million, it would be the most expensive Mexican film ever made. There was outright opposition from a Mexican film industry who thought genre films were beneath

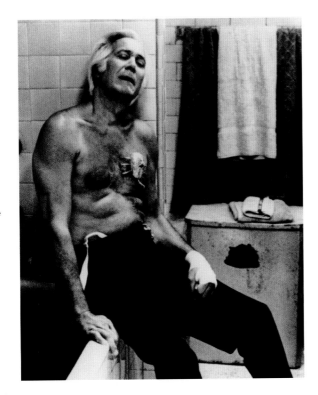

them. They told Bertha she was mad. State funding went to art, not crazy ideas about vampires and insects and eerie children. The tone was bewildering. Was this a tale of family devotion or a horror story? Del Toro was even proposing casting the revered Argentinian actor Federico Luppi in the lead role.

Casting was imperative. This wasn't a slasher movie. Del Toro's 'strange poetic flavour'[42] would be found in the characters. He had loved Luppi in the existential hitman thriller *Last Days of the Victim* (1982), in which he managed to convey powerful emotions with minimal dialogue. Even at 59, Luppi had the expressive body language of Keaton and that same natural melancholy. So fixed was del Toro on casting the 'Argentinian Olivier,'[43] he had already pictured him in the storyboards. Furthermore, the fates had decreed that just at that moment, Luppi was in Mexico to make a film. Del Toro negotiated his way onto set, knocked on his dressing room door, and handed him the script.

The actor saw that the story was filled with darkness, yet often very funny. At a New Year's Eve party designed almost in monochrome, the prissy antiquarian he was being asked to portray watches, rapt, as a fellow guest staunches a nosebleed, leaving a single scarlet splash on the tiled floor of the bathroom. In the film's signature image, the reluctant vampire laps at the blood like a cat.

'I wanted him to be alive only after he dies,'[44] said del Toro. The more he gives himself to the Cronos Device, the younger Jesús Gris appears, and the more gregarious his moods.

More significant even than Luppi was the distinctive American character actor del Toro persuaded to head south of the border to play sardonic heavy Angel.

An American investor had suggested that, if they cast an American, he would be more conducive to contributing a vital $600,000 to the budget. Originally, del Toro had conceived of Angel and his uncle as Nazis gone to ground in Mexico, and had pictured them being played by European icons Klaus Maria Brandauer and Max von Sydow. But he was more than ready to compromise. Making the enemy a cartoonish American would be revenge for the endless Mexican thugs in American movies.

Angel, at least, is a brute with a heart. He accepts violence as a wearisome inevitability of his employment. He is another misunderstood monster, heavy on the cynicism – a trial run for *Hellboy*. All of which drew del Toro straight to the entry in his encyclopaedic brain on Ron Perlman. With the barrel chest and spade-like jawline of a comic-book mobster, and piercing, sensitive blue eyes, the classically trained actor from Washington Heights tended to stand out. He also came with a voice like a cave-in. He was as much a weather front as an actor, and simply beautiful to del Toro – who had adored him as, respectively, caveman and demented

monk in *Quest for Fire* and *The Name of the Rose*.

For his part, Perlman was enthralled by the screenplay. Even more so by the accompanying handwritten 'love letter'[45] from del Toro eulogizing his previous performances. 'Never in a million years would it ever get greenlit in Hollywood,' he thought. 'And just for that reason alone, I'm going to fucking do it.'[46]

The casting of de la Guardia, the film's cold-hearted variation on germophobe billionaire Howard Hughes, was also not without significance. For del Toro chose Claudio

Brook, star of *The Exterminating Angel* and *Simon of the Desert*, and Buñuel's favourite Mexican actor.

Beginning in February 1992, Cronos was made during eight traumatic weeks in Mexico City. Del Toro was 29. 'Any film is hard to do,' he reflected. 'The first one is no exception. It was a very gruelling ordeal. The best and worst of times: I was fructifying a project that I cherished for eight years but being financially screwed.'[47]

Halfway through, the money ran out. Their vaunted American investor turned out to be a charlatan. Del Toro was left, by his own account, trying 'crazy and desperate'[48] measures to save his film. First, he faced Perlman. 'I can't pay you now,' he implored, 'but I promise you *will* get paid.'[49] If he lost his American star, the production was doomed. Against his agent's wishes, Perlman agreed to stay on. That set the seal on a lifelong friendship. He would get his money, and there would be even greater dividends for the actor down the line. He could see this baby-faced Mexican dude was a born filmmaker. From the first day, it was like he had been doing it his whole life.

Del Toro took out a loan on his house, sold his car, and hawked possessions. Anything to keep his strange dream afloat. They would end up paying another half a million in interest. It took four years to get his house back in his own name. One of the reasons he hastily signed on to make *Mimic* as his next film was to pay his debts. 'I have to make films…'[50] he insisted, like an addict or a vampire. Money would always be secondary to art: he put half his salary back into *Hellboy*, paid for special effects shots in *Mimic* and *Blade II* out of his own pocket, and forswore a fee on *Pan's Labyrinth* to sate his ravenous hunger for movies.

Opposite: A friendship born out of tribulation – the lifelong bond between del Toro and actor Ron Perlman began when the American stuck by him during the budget problems on *Cronos*.

Above: Claudio Brook as the villainous de la Guardia. This reclusive billionaire hungry for immortality was loosely based on Howard Hughes. Notice too, the emergence of drapes as a signature motif.

Even in post-production, problems lay in wait. Del Toro had shifted to Los Angeles to make use of digital facilities absent from Mexico. Forget the deluxe Hollywood lifestyle: he was staying in a three-hundred-dollar-a-month hotel with problem plumbing. He had to go to another hotel every three days in order to shower. 'Or I could have a hot dog at Pink's,' he recalled. 'Those were my choices. The day I took a shower, I couldn't eat lunch.'[51]

He was struggling to make sense of his film. The first cut was long-winded. It lacked that essential flow. Cuarón gave it to him straight – cut twenty-five minutes. And he was still sweating on effects shots that have the camera peer into the Cronos Device. The illusion was created using a large-scale model based on designs from del Toro's notebooks, where cogs and gears are seen revolving in close-up along with glimpses of the (never explained) immortal insect pulsating at its core. He had to keep space free in his edit, praying to whichever god might listen that they would come through on time.

His desperation bled into *Cronos* and gave it life. The completed film is a singular marvel. Even within his modest budget, this was imagery worthy of Buñuel. '*Cronos* represents a filmmaker joyously conducting a symphony of tone interlocking with cinematic details,'[52] wrote Glenn Heath Jr. in *Slant Magazine*. Design and storytelling were entwined like branches in a vine. How fitting that Jesús Gris would be an obtainer of rare antiquities, for it granted leave for del Toro to fill each scene to the gills with symbols and props – all the fetishized paraphernalia of his imagination. Here are the staples of that rich del Toro look: baroque contraptions, specimens in murky jars, fusty rooms piled with relics and tomes. Signature motifs emerged that would reoccur across his work. He called it 'rhyming.'[53] This was the first sighting of a flamboyant directorial handwriting where everything you see and hear carries layers of interconnected meaning like an archaeological dig.

Take the Cronos Device itself. It is the shape of an egg, denoting eternity and immortality. Notice too, how Jesús Gris's head begins to peel like an egg, revealing a milky white surface beneath. The scarab is a major part of the Egyptian concept of the afterlife.

Left: The precious and deadly Cronos Device, first in a line of clockwork mechanisms of all sizes that will drive the engines of his stories to come.

Carved into its golden carapace is the shape of a serpent eating its tail – immortality again. And the Möbius strip that encircles the device, del Toro's touch, stands for infinity.

The director accepted that such a 'symbolic reading'[54] may only be for him, but he loved how there was a secret code embedded into his film. 'You would hopefully always see new things on returning to the films,'[55] he said. *Cronos* seeps into your system.

So after a modest release, making $621,000 worldwide, the film would gradually earn the cult reputation it was due (and slowly eke out a profit). With some satisfaction, del Toro and his team won nine Silver Ariels, the Mexican version of the Oscars, including Best Direction, Best Screenplay and Best First Work. Internationally too, the film gained a precious berth at the Cannes Film Festival, and won the Critics' Week Award. That got him noticed by American producers. And yet, when

Universal asked about the English language remake rights to *Cronos*, del Toro was baffled. 'Who wants see Jack Lemmon lick the bathroom floor?'[56] He torpedoed the idea on the spot. Some stories belong to Mexico.

Looking back, a wiser man, he can see the film's shortcomings. 'The screenplay was much better than the film, I think, and I would have done a lot of things differently. But each movie is a portrait of the moment you made it in. And to me *Cronos* still has a lot of qualities.'[57]

In 1993, a few months after the release, del Toro was invited to Madrid. To his delight, he found that *Cronos* was still playing in midnight screenings at the Salsa Princesa cinema. Naturally, he went that night. How could he resist? Rather than the film, he found himself watching this guy, sat a couple of rows in front of him, whispering lines before the characters even said them. He was clearly addicted.

Above: As the movie was celebrated in various film festivals, the young del Toro thrilled to the chance to see the world beyond Mexico.

TUNNEL VISION

Mimic (1997)

How a first, bitter encounter with Hollywood almost crushed his spirit, but ultimately gave him the determination to forge his own path, and gave the world a giant bug movie whose reputation keeps on growing

In the depths of the New York subway, dank and rusty as a shipwreck, giant insects are plotting dominion. Chittering like wind-up teeth, they are the result of scientific hubris. A *Frankenstein* tune can be heard beneath the monster-movie formula. The Judas Breed is a genetically supercharged species of cockroach designed to wipe out its regular cousins. We learn that the roaches carried a deadly plague that struck only the city's children. Which is very Biblical. They were programmed to die off; however, three years later, they have not only survived, but evolved. Shadowy, human-shaped figures are roving the streets like villains from a film noir with their hands stuffed into their pockets and collars raised, while making a fierce clicking sound. People are going missing. Weird shit is going down – quite literally, when the camera slowly tracks out to reveal a room forested in insect turds. Those responsible – entomologist Dr. Susan Tyler (Mira Sorvino) and her disease control agent husband Dr. Peter Mann (Jeremy Northam) – head down into the dark to make amends.

Above: As the poster for Guillermo del Toro's much troubled *Mimic* attests, the film actually garnered some decent reviews.

Right: Mira Sorvino's Dr. Susan Tyler makes an early sortie into the infested subways of New York – del Toro's first great labyrinth.

This is the fictional backdrop to a genuine nightmare. The salutary tale of Guillermo's del Toro's second film – into which he was lured like a fly caught in a web called Miramax.

On the subject of *Mimic*, del Toro tends not to mince his words. 'It was a horrible, horrible, horrible experience,'[1] he said, followed by a deep, steadying breath. He cannot point to one single day on *Mimic* that was pleasant. His irresistible personal vision met an immovable object – Bob Weinstein (from hereon simply Bob), younger brother of the notorious Harvey Weinstein, who ruled over Miramax's genre-orientated label Dimension

Likewise, Bob was a man of ferocious temperament, regarding his directors – especially those he viewed as having been plucked from obscurity, thanks to his largesse – as being there to facilitate the company's requirements as cheaply as possible.

Producer B.J. Rack, who took her share of the flak in trying to intercede between director and studio, was every bit as frank. 'I've worked with Paul Verhoeven and I've produced a Jim Cameron movie, but *Mimic* is the hardest professional experience I have ever had. I felt like I was in a prisoner-of-war camp.'[2]

All this, you might ask, over a giant bug picture? But for del Toro there is no such thing as just a giant bug picture.

Mimic had begun life with more modest ambitions. It was developed by Miramax as one-third of a triptych

Below: Guillermo del Toro saw *Mimic* as an opportunity to pay homage to Gordon Douglas's spectacular *Them!* in which giant ants emerge from the sewers.

Opposite: The poster for *Them!* played up the typical sensationalism of 1950s science fiction - a B-movie fervour that del Toro would subtly inject into his darker tales.

of science-fiction stories collectively entitled *Light Years*, each to be directed by an exciting new talent: Gary Fleder, Danny Boyle, and del Toro – who had fallen under the beady eyes of the Weinsteins after his reputation had been sung around the festival circuit thanks to *Cronos*. Adapted by Matthew Robbins from a short story by Donald A. Wollheim, the script pre-dated del Toro's arrival. Two of the stories – *Mimic*, and Fleder's Philip K. Dick adaptation *Impostor* – were soon considered worthy of stand-alone feature films. Boyle's *Alien Love Triangle* was made as a short and shelved forevermore.

The appeal of *Mimic* to del Toro was obvious. Creepy-crawlies lie close to his heart. On his very first trip to New York as a kid, he bought a giant replica of a bug. He still has it framed at home, the inspiration for insect-like creatures in *Pan's Labyrinth* and *Hellboy II: The Golden Army*. Mexico is a country of bugs; you learned to live with them. Del Toro became fixated on how they appear to be engineered.

'They are the true living automatons of nature,'[3] he said, awe-struck with how they evoked a strange parallel between machines and life. What are humans, he often ponders in films filled with autopsies, transformations, and robotic simulacra, if not organic machines? What is it that makes us different? We fear insects because of their 'lack of emotion,'[4] he concluded. The hive mind (from fascism to Hollywood) will crush the soul.

With giant ants loose in its sewers, del Toro considers *Them!* to be the greatest mutant insect film ever made – and he is exactly the kind of guy to have a favourite mutant insect film. All in all, the low concept of mutant cockroaches amassing beneath New York was a dream come true. Only now that it had been upgraded to a full-length Hollywood feature film, things got sticky in the wrong sense.

There were disputes over the expanded script, casting, design and budget. Del Toro was still too naïve to comprehend that this was the Miramax way: the two brothers in a state of

near-constant fury. Especially with Bob, it was a process of beating his directors into submission: he would press and bully, then allow a brief lull, fooling them into thinking they were onto something, then demand another rewrite, and another.

Bob would preside over story meetings that could last for eleven or twelve hours. They were held in the conference room in Miramax's Tribeca offices in New York, whose frosted glass walls and hothouse atmosphere led victims to dub it the Sweatbox. Line by line, he would pick apart the script. Every original notion, anything idiosyncratic, was slowly, surely whittled away.

In hindsight, using Peter Biskind's unblinkered history of the Miramax era *Down and Dirty Pictures* as a guide, what Bob may have had in mind was an *Alien* knock-off, a B-picture, shock and gore on the New York commute. Del Toro was indeed reaching for the auspices of *Alien*, but he was thinking more of Ridley Scott's handling of atmosphere and his dense, clammy

Above: The bug hunters are cornered in a disused subway carriage. *From left:* Charles S. Dutton, Giancarlo Giannini, Sorvino, and Jeremy Hunt confront the super-sized cockroaches.

design. 'I think that the eighties British directors like Adrian Lyne, Alan Parker and, towering above all, Ridley Scott have been a major example of how the lens can become a clean, sharp instrument to dissect the world,'[5] he commented in a cooler moment.

'Are you making an art movie?'[6] demanded Bob. Del Toro made his case that art and bugs can be one and the same. The movie needed to look sumptuous. It needed emotional sense.

His words spilled into the void.

Perhaps what Bob actually wanted was the *Sturm und Drang* thrills of *Aliens*. The second-half of *Mimic*, with the scientists, seasoned transit cop (Charles S. Dutton), and a small, autistic child Chuy (Alexander Goodwin), cornered deep underground in an old subway car, moves to a similar beat. Del Toro

sneered that what they ended up with was more like *'Alien 3 and a Half.'*[7]

Once he was shooting in Toronto (with a little guile, a cost-effective stand-in for New York), Bob's furies still rang in his ears. Through the winter of 1996, as the sub-zero Canadian temperatures delivered their own culture shock, Bob would call. Bob would scream. Bob would watch the dailies and call again, demanding more action, more chases, and more goddam explosions!

Del Toro tried to keep his head. When forced by Miramax to change his creatures from elegant tree beetles to cockroaches, he resolved – paraphrasing his own words on the Blu-ray extras – to make the best damn giant cockroach movie he could. But Bob's attacks were a form of gaslighting. Del Toro couldn't fathom the endless instructions being hurled at him, and felt like he was going mad. He knew the film he wanted to make, he could see it, feel it, and was genuinely excited about the possibilities.

There were rare victories for the Mexican storyteller. During one of the many production meetings, he was told that Miramax strictly prohibited the depiction of any violence against animals or children, so he went ahead and filmed a scene where two children and a dog die. 'I don't know if this is much of an achievement but it felt like one,'[8] he recalled, clutching at small mercies. The scene is merciless, with children falling prey to razor-sharp pincers – an early warning that he could be a very dark filmmaker indeed.

A smaller thing, but del Toro loved that he managed to have

Northam's scientist wear glasses that get cracked like Piggy's in *Lord of the Flies*. Broken glasses are a potent symbol of man's frailty.

But other thrilling ideas were squashed beneath Bob's heel. Central to del Toro's original conception was the revelation that these super-sized insects are the vanguard of a rethink by God. In a dash of Old Testament fury, the deity plans to wipe the board clean and start again with sentient bugs to the fore.

'So the true villain in the screenplay I wrote was God,'[9] he stressed. All that remains of his overarching theme are a few gimmicky gestures. The killing of a priest by roaches at the very beginning takes place in the rundown church beneath a huge sign declaring 'Jesus saves!'

Del Toro had a terrifying ending in store. The male of the Judas Breed would survive and stand over Sorvino revealing a perfect facsimile of a human face, then point with a perfect-looking human digit, and finally speak, 'Leave!'[10] The idea that the insects had become sentient chilled him to the bone. He lost that battle too.

'All that remains there is like vulture leftovers…'[11] grimaced del Toro.

While casting decisions were often taken out of his hands, he spoke warmly of the friendship he developed, under great stress, with Northam and, as would prove vital, Sorvino. A plan to cast his old friend Federico Luppi from *Cronos* as the subway shoe-shiner Manny was scuppered when the actor's English pronunciation wouldn't stretch. The Italian actor Giancarlo

Left: Mira Sorvino investigates some unpleasantly overgrown remains – a shot that shows the development of del Toro's 'nighttime look' with deep, ink blues punctuated by splashes of amber.

Giannini replaced him. Manny's autistic grandson is all that is left of a subplot about a class of sewer-dwelling mole people, passive humans who have come to love their cockroach masters.

Bob was not to be swayed by the moody, probing, far-reaching thriller that was taking shape, bearing the hallmarks of Ridley Scott and early David Fincher (whose *Seven* was another significant touchstone). Eventually, the fulminating executive began visiting the set in person, sitting twenty or so feet from the camera and del Toro, with Rack acting as his intermediary. Bob would loudly issue a command – and virtually every shot was called into question – and Rack would have to scamper up to her director and relay what del Toro had

undoubtedly already heard. Bob had no sense of boundaries. All del Toro could do was to keep going.

'I remember there was a moment on *Mimic* that was an almost out-of-body experience, when I achieved an absolute Taoist sense of being there, but being almost in a state of grace and being able to survive that fucking pain.'[12]

In what began to resemble (figuratively at least) one of *Hellboy's* never-ending punch-ups, Bob then sent in his own second unit director to provide extra scenes as he wanted them: lumps of gaudy action that made little effort to match the precision of del Toro's colour scheme, slowly swelling mood, or subtle teasing of horrors outside of the camera's view. And still, having examined an assembly

of footage, Bob threw another seismic tantrum. As far as he was concerned, the time had come to fire del Toro. According to Biskind's account, he lined up Danish director Ole Bornedal (who had remade his own *Nightwatch* for Dimension) as a replacement, or possibly Robert Rodriguez. Given that Bornedal receives an executive producer credit, we can assume it was he who ran the Bob-mandated second unit.

Director and mogul met in a hotel room. 'You're not the right guy,'[13] Bob told him. He would be on the first flight out that evening. Del Toro was left in a state of shock, fearing for his career. But it wasn't over yet. Sorvino was waiting down in the lobby, unaware she was now bereft of a director.

Right: Sorvino's bug specialist confronts the truth that her tampering with nature resulted in the killer strain – a theme del Toro drew directly from *Frankenstein*.

Opposite below: Del Toro was seeking some of the sophistication of David Cronenberg's modern insect mutation classic *The Fly* – they even share the same production designer in Carol Spier.

Despite recently winning an Oscar with Miramax for *Mighty Aphrodite*, Sorvino had plenty to lose in taking on the might of the Weinsteins, who were at the height of their power. 'It was a time where they were kind of golden in the industry,' said del Toro, trying to make sense of how they got away with such tactics, 'so that anything that went wrong at Miramax was your fault, not theirs.'[14]

To her eternal credit, Sorvino didn't think twice. Taking one look at an ashen del Toro, she saw immediately what was going on. Before Bob could say anything, she unleashed a furious, expletive-laden tirade in his direction, refusing to return to set unless del Toro was reinstated. She also had a secret weapon. At the time, she was dating Quentin Tarantino – Miramax's golden boy. He had visited the set on a number of occasions, enjoying del Toro's company. Tarantino put in a placatory call, knowing full well that Sorvino wouldn't have done the film if not for *Cronos*. She was buying into del Toro's vision. Bob was finally forced to back down and allow del Toro to finish *Mimic*. Though he would retain final cut.

Even compared to his trials on *Cronos*, del Toro was spiritually crushed by the experience. He was still young, only 32, though pictures show a youthful pallor that could belong to a teenager – an uncorrupted soul not yet equipped for the monsters of Hollywood. There were nights when he wondered whether he was cut out for making movies. Not if it was going to be like this.

'Hollywood,' he said, 'isn't like a wave, something you stand up to, pure of heart. It's mildew. It sort of permeates a wall slowly until it rots and only by the time it's falling on you do you realize what it is. It's perverse, slow and deliberate.'[15]

But here's the thing, and this is an enduring testament to the strength of del Toro's eye in adversity: even in its original, hogtied form, *Mimic* is a half-decent horror movie. As Owen Gleiberman of *Entertainment Weekly* commented, for all the rattling formula, we are left in a 'constant state of kinesthetic anxiety.'[16]

Yes, it lurches about unevenly, with large lapses of interior logic, but there is discernible style. One of the few blessings was that del Toro had got to work with Carol Spier, production designer on ten of David Cronenberg's films. With his strain of intellectual body horror, Cronenberg was another big influence, and a director to whom he has often been compared. 'I think Cronenberg is existential whereas I'm romantic,'[17] countered del Toro, but *The Fly* looms large over *Mimic*.

Staggering uphill, out of breath, bearing the weight of the studio demands, del Toro still created a dank, evocative atmosphere that is identifiably his trademark. Roger Ebert, reviewing the film and not the furore, divined a director who has 'a way of drawing us into his story and evoking the mood with the very look and texture of his shots.'[18] In terms of colour, here are those saturated amber highlights against pools of inky blacks and blues. Here is the first outing

for motifs that would emerge again and again: the knots of subterranean passages; the torrential rain; and the gothic tableaux of statuary, like the sculptures in the ramshackle chapel wrapped in polythene.

And it is in *Mimic* that del Toro first revealed his supremacy in the creation of monsters. There is something uniquely del Toro-esque in the genre-bending concept of six-foot insects mimicking human form. They have character.

Despite its painful birth and limp returns at the box office ($25 million), the film has grown in favour. We can classify it as the cult del Toro, the awkward child. Remarkably, two sequels have been made, and a television series has been mooted. None of which del Toro has had anything to do with.

More valuably, in 2011, with the Weinsteins long departed and del Toro's reputation soaring, he was given the chance to re-edit his footage into something like a *Director's Cut*, as it would be classified, but still hardly the film he set out to make. Out went all the second-unit crap, all those mindless attempts to soup up the action. Now it was only first-unit crap, he quipped, with an additional seven minutes of his footage. If you don't like it, it's on him. A worthy film emerges from the ugly chrysalis, with a chance for del Toro to set the record straight in the DVD extras.

Themes are resurrected. Here is that *Frankenstein* story, or as del Toro put it in less literary mood, the idea 'to have a yuppie couple fuck with nature and then, a few years later, get the shaft in a major way.'[19]

The hospital scene that opens the *Director's Cut* carries all of del Toro's warped fairy-tale language: the ward looks like it belongs in a cathedral, with each of the beds, occupied by sick children, covered in a translucent canopy and splashes of golden light. In the eerie gloom they appear to be cocoons. Close observers will notice the similarity with de la Guardia's hermetic chamber in *Cronos*. Bob was certainly not a member of that select club. The strange paradox of Miramax was that they wanted to be seen as innovators, promoting vibrant new talent, only to do their utmost to dull such individuality once they got to work. Bob could only fume – this isn't what hospitals looked like in the real world.

Patterns shared with *Cronos* become more apparent in the *Director's Cut*. The shoe-shiner and his silent grandson recall Jesús Gris and his wordless granddaughter. Maybe not to the extent he had planned, but the spectre of religion still hangs over the film. It regains a mordant sense of humour. There is family drama as the lead couple struggle to conceive, suggesting karmic payback. 'Somehow because of the additions the film feels better paced and less rushed,'[20] noticed *Starburst*.

Left: Stars Jeremy Northam and Mira Sorvino examine evidence that the mutant roaches have evolved to mimic human form – Guillermo del Toro's original idea was for the creatures to ultimately reveal that they are sentient.

Below: Character actor F. Murray Abraham as Sorvino's mentor Dr. Gates, whose chief purpose in the plot is to deliver portentous truths to the heroine and audience about the morality of science.

Opposite: One of Guillermo del Toro's beautiful notebooks in close-up. Within it we can discern intricate designs and notes for *Pan's Labyrinth*, including sketches for the Pale Man and the mandrake root baby.

Left: The dead foetus of a giant insect, revealing hints of a human form. Inspired by a visit to a Mexican hospital as a young man, foetuses will reoccur across his work.

It was during the promotion of *Mimic* that del Toro's remarkable notebooks first came to light. He was doing a television interview with Sorvino and mentioned how he ritually maps out his ideas in pen and ink on the pages of leather-bound notebooks that he always carries with him. 'Show him,'[21] Sorvino had pressed, and reluctantly del Toro handed over his current notebook to the host, terrified he would leave a smudge.

This process of archiving his brainwaves began when an early mentor, Mexican screenwriter Jaime Humberto Hermosillo, insisted he keep notes. They evolved from tape recordings to spiral pads, and eventually to the luxury notebooks he keeps in his bag or jacket pocket.

Now running into their hundreds (and once filled, carefully stored away), they are a physical representation of the thought process applied to his films from the earliest stages. Across these pages, as beautifully cluttered as da Vinci's *Codex*, you can see him setting down sparks of inspiration, teasing out problems, conceiving shots, and mingling ideas to create something

new. All the motifs, those gimcrack mechanisms, tentacled horrors, engorged mouths, and weird eyes, spill from page to page, and from film to film. There are random memories, lines of dialogue, and tiny masterpieces of marginalia. As he described them, they are 'a testament to curiosity.'[22]

Besides, they are a really effective way to communicate to actors and designers. 'I also do the first breakdown of colours here, both for the art direction and the lighting,'[23] he said. You could say these books are an art project unto themselves, in which he has elaborated his penmanship to resemble the touch of a quill, and drawn wonderful, expressive pictures. Each one is as weathered as a prop. Indeed, you'll see similar notebooks appear in the hands of many of his characters. One day he will pass them onto to his daughters as a legacy.

'I want them to remain intact so they can give them to their children in turn,' he reflected, 'or else just browse through them and see how deranged their father was.'[24]

James Cameron, who had got to know del Toro while he was in

post on *Cronos*, watched the young man's increasing frustration as he navigated the treacherous waters of Hollywood, but ultimately came out with his head held high. 'He tried to apply his old-world Latin honour to a business in which honour is as alien and abstract as calculus to a fish,'[25] he observed, and one of the things Cameron so admires about del Toro is how, despite everything, he has stayed true to that code.

With the dust long since settled on *Mimic*, del Toro can take a philosophical, if-it-doesn't-kill-you attitude toward the hardships he endured and the film (or films) that emerged. He can honestly say that he came away a better filmmaker.

'I learned to make my camera more fluid, more a storytelling character; it really helped me develop the language that I [still practised] on *The Shape Of Water*. It taught me to edit every day because I was always expecting to be fired. I'll have a cut of the movie six days after wrap. I think adversity is good...'

He paused for a moment, and then smiled. 'That is very Catholic of me.'[26]

UNFINISHED BUSINESS
The Devil's Backbone (2001)

How his third film, an intimate ghost story set in a lonely orphanage
amid the Spanish Civil War, defined his style, made his reputation,
and revealed a filmmaker using genre to explore the world

With *The Devil's Backbone*, Guillermo del Toro comes of age. Here is the first full expression of his themes: that literary slant to his storytelling, his enquiry into the darkest shades of human nature, the juxtaposition of violence and myth. Many fans, especially early disciples, see it as still the finest expression of del Toro's gifts. He might well agree. 'Depending on the week,' he has said, 'I like it as much or more than *Pan's Labyrinth*, never less.'[1]

Set in a remote orphanage in a parched landscape, it is a politically inclined ghost story with the Spanish Civil War as its backdrop. Within a film of great beauty and heartbreak, images press indelibly from his imagination into yours. The glimpses of a ghostly boy, whispering in the corridors, blood perpetually bubbling from a head wound as if he was submerged. The shot of a drowning man, weighed down by the stolen gold attached to his belt. The deformed foetuses with twisted backbones preserved in jars of fluid as bright as orangeade. And most striking of all, a huge, unexploded bomb planted nose-down in the central courtyard like a monument.

'The bomb is an immense emblem of the film's undetonated power,' wrote critic Matt Zoller Seitz, 'likened in dialogue to a fertility goddess.'[2] Del Toro referred to it as the mother of the orphaned boys. They worship it, he said, 'like the head of the pig in *Lord of the Flies*.'[3] We too are instantly drawn to its pregnant symbolism. For this is a film of unfinished business, written in the midst of the biggest crisis of del Toro's life.

Above: Both the headmistress Carmen (Marisa Paredes) and unlikeable caretaker Jacinto (Eduardo Noriega) have their secrets. Behind them stands the symbolically unexploded bomb.

Right: The literally haunting features of the ghost Santi (Junio Valverde) literally framed (or trapped) within the blurred windowpane.

He was back in Guadalajara, licking his wounds after *Mimic*, and wondering what the future might hold – wondering if he had a future at all. He needed to reassert his independence, almost to begin again. *Cronos* had turned out well enough, but the scrambling for budget was exhausting. *Mimic* had a budget, but left him trapped inside the fortress of Miramax, his creativity in shackles. And now, after his bug movie had gone legs up at the box office, studios were keeping their distance.

'I desperately needed to go back and do a movie [where] I had absolute control over the material,' he reflected. 'And I also wanted to prove to myself that I could do my own stories.'[4]

The answer lay in a script that dated back to his student days (at one stage as part of his thesis) and, quite by chance, took on a new lease of life.

In October 1997, two young Spanish critics, Antonio Trashorras and David Mũnoz, sought out del Toro at the Sitges International Fantastic Film Festival, held a few miles up the Catalonian coast from Barcelona. They immediately bonded over a shared love of comics and movies, with the two Spaniards drawn into the natural largesse of the Mexican's enthusiasm. That was when they took the chance to solicit his opinion on five screenplays they had with them. This side effect of his growing prominence tended to fill del Toro with dread. There was every chance the scripts might be awful. 'Oh my God,' he thought, 'what am I going to say?'[5]

Predictably, he didn't like four of them at all. But the fifth, entitled *The Bomb*, had this captivating image of an unexploded bomb, delivered from on high to this isolated orphanage, something he could see straightaway in his mind's eye. Two months later he had bought the rights, and suggested

they collaborate on fusing their stories into an updated version of *The Devil's Backbone*.

Trashorras and Mũnoz's screenplay was located somewhere cold and desolate, an ambiguous zone not unlike the setting for Andrei Tarkovsky's *Stalker*. The walls of the orphanage were medieval. The bomb was more directly a conduit for the supernatural. Del Toro would bring the specificity of history. His original milieu, the Mexican Revolution, was too messy, too factionalized. 'I wanted the war to be a war that happened within a family, an intimate war where brothers killed brothers.'[6] That took him straight to the Spanish Civil War.

Mexico is, of course, a child of Spain. The Spanish conquistadors had infused the new nation with the culture and language of the Old World. That link, a collective memory of a motherland across the ocean, has never broken. Mexico was one of the few countries to accept refugees

from the Spanish Civil War: the intellectuals, artists and schoolteachers who fled Franco. Del Toro would channel the voice of those exiles back into Spain.

The year is 1939, and as the war rages in the distance, a small, sensitive boy named Carlos (Fernando Tielve) arrives at the Santa Lucia orphanage, which stands alone like a fortress in the Tabernas Desert. In the central quadrangle looms that totemic bomb dropped by a German squadron – a constant reminder, if the orphans needed one, of the conflict.

In his research, del Toro found that the Germans were testing blanket bombing in Spain at this time. His bomb is bigger than would have been the case, but he was thinking along the lines of the surreal lunacy of Kubrick's *Dr. Strangelove*. 'To hell with it,' he said to himself. 'It's a great image.'[7] The panoptic shot of the explosive descending through clouds and rain – similar

Above: Guillermo del Toro wanted to use the gang of young boys in this remote orphanage to show how the innocence of Spain was corrupted by the rise of fascism.

Opposite: At the beginning of the film, the distraught Carlos (Fernando Tielve) is left behind at the orphanage – supposedly for his own safety. But there is no escape from the winds of war.

storms will clog the skies of films to come – transforms the mechanics of war into an agent of destiny.

Carlos will encounter a clique of unruly boys, and a ghostly outsider, Santi or 'The One Who Sighs' (Junio Valverde), a terrifying apparition with skin as white as a fish, who comes to meet the new arrival on his first night. Del Toro would remind interviewers that he had spent his childhood as a 'pale introspective creature of the shadows.'[8]

He would also introduce more adult concerns. Kindly, impotent Professor Casares (Federico Luppi from *Cronos*), who runs the orphanage, mixes rum with the fluid from his collection of embalmed foetuses to sell as a reviving elixir. The bitter headmistress Carmen (Marisa Paredes), who has lost a leg and husband to

the war, secretes gold bars for the Republican cause inside her prosthetic limb. And the handsome but heartless caretaker Jacinto (Eduardo Noriega) yearns to burn it all to the ground and make off with the hidden treasure.

Del Toro and his collaborators had only begun to get to grips with this new alloy of their mutual ideas when the worst happened. In 1997, del Toro's father was kidnapped. He would be held for a heartrending seventy-two days.

If this is a personal detail, a family matter, there is no avoiding the profound effect it had on the filmmaker's art. His early rise to prominence had suggested to potential kidnappers he was far wealthier than was the case. He had barely paid back his debts on *Cronos*. Cementing their friendship in ways that went vastly beyond professional kinship, James Cameron would pay to hire a specialist negotiator.

Del Toro has been remarkably candid about the events that followed, relaying them with the practised art of a storyteller. 'The first day you think you're going to die,' he said. 'The second day, you're absolutely certain you won't survive. The third day, you cry at the drop of a hat because you think this is hell… You are a hostage to the hostage situation.'[9]

In encapsulating the ordeal, we can never truly catch the excruciating, prolonged agony involved. And the strangeness. For instance, the ransom money was literally made up of fives and ones because that was all that the bank in Guadalajara had in the vault. Half a million dollars in fives and ones, which had be photocopied by hand so the police would have a record. The first man hired to deliver the ransom lost his nerve, and del Toro was forced to carry the money himself. On a plane that came emblazoned in police decals. When the kidnappers provided the coordinates, it turned out the pilot had no idea how to navigate by numbers. The kidnappers had to call back and direct them toward a range of mountains. Then there was too much fog to land, and del Toro had to call the maddened kidnappers once more.

Every conversation with them is heralded by a litany of abuse, designed to keep him off guard. They tell him to land and get a car. But he can't do that or he'll be taken. Life and death seem to hang in the electrical static on the line. Eventually, after further fraught calls, the original delivery guy is convinced to make the drop, and del Toro's father is finally released unharmed.

With characteristic gallows humour, the director still considered *Mimic* the worse of his two life-

changing traumas. 'The kidnapping made more sense, I knew what they wanted.'[10]

In the midst of all this, the negotiator advised him to keep working, stick to his routine, and not make himself a target. Coincidentally (or indeed symbolically) he had also been commissioned to adapt *The Count of Monte Cristo*, perhaps the most famous tale of confinement ever written, and his father's favourite book. Life and art began to bleed into one another.

Del Toro methodically divided his time. In the mornings he wrote *The Count of Monte Cristo* (with American writer Kit Carson), spicing up Alexandre Dumas's epic of Restoration France with a Spaghetti Western flavour. He retitled it *The Left Hand of Darkness* (lifted from an unrelated Ursula K. Le Guin story) and gave the Count a mechanical hand as ornate as the *Cronos* device. At one particularly fraught juncture of his father's kidnap, the kidnappers had screamed at del Toro to get the delivery of the ransom right, 'or when you get home you're

gonna find your father's hands in the fucking doorway waiting for you.'[11]

The Left Hand of Darkness is one in a list of unmade projects that haunt his thoughts like unrequited loves. We'll come back to the legacy of these ghost films in a later chapter. For now, it's worth noting that Carlos has a well-thumbed copy of the Dumas original in *The Devil's Backbone*, and there is a lovely, leather-bound copy in Professor Bruttenholm's library in *Hellboy*.

The afternoons del Toro devoted to *The Devil's Backbone*. It became a kind of purging. 'A film about ghosts cleared all ghosts from my past,'[12] he said.

To survive with his sanity intact from this combination of professional and personal trauma gave him a foundation for the future. *The Devil's Backbone* resonates with the authority of an artist who has passed through a baptism by fire.

In using a form as familiar as the ghost story, del Toro intends to reconnect his chosen genre with its thematic roots in order to create something new. 'The vampire film, the

Opposite: Jacinto (Eduardo Noriega) serves as a brutal role model for the boys, especially the impressionable Jaime (Íñigo Garcés).

Below: The afterlife after dark - Carlos (Fernando Tielve) has his first terrifying nighttime encounter with the ghost of Santi.

ghost story, and the fairy-tale are re-elaborated in my work, rather than just re-enacted or imitated,'[13] he explained.

'What is a ghost?' asks Casares in voice-over. 'A tragedy condemned to repeat itself time and time again? An instance of pain, perhaps. Something dead which still seems to be alive. An emotion suspended in time. Like a blurred photograph. Like an insect trapped in amber.'[14]

In relocating to Spain, the film had gained a stark political dimension. Fascism, del Toro iterated, was the ultimate perversion of innocence – symbolized in the film by childhood. It would become a recurring theme: *Hellboy*, *Pan's Labyrinth*, and *The Shape of Water* all dip into history's poisoned well.

Counter to that, William Golding's *Lord of the Flies* – with its feral boys regressing to antediluvian savagery – was a guiding light. Spain, del Toro recognized, had become the equivalent of the desert island; as is the orphanage, cut off from the world. By the end, its young residents are sharpening spears to defend themselves.

He knew in his bones that this was a film that could never be made with a studio. They would have flinched at the violence inflicted by and toward children. 'But that's the core of the movie,' he insisted: 'it has to show children as mortal figures.'[15] He also intended to shoot it in authentic Spanish.

So the question arose of how he was going to raise the budget. Local

Left: As a sneering Jacinto (Eduardo Noriega) looks on, Jaime (Íñigo Garcés) bestows a ring to the object of his youthful crush – the orphanage's pretty hired hand Conchita (Irene Visedo).

Below: However, Conchita has already given her heart to the heartless Jacinto – another refraction of Spain falling under the spell of fascism.

Opposite: At first, Carlos (Fernando Tielve) is excluded from the intimate circle of boys – a classic representative of Guillermo del Toro's outcast heroes.

funding was another blind alley. *Cronos* may have been garlanded with awards, but the Mexican Institute of Film remained sceptical about del Toro's strange stories. Besides, he was informed, 'it was too big a movie.'[16] With the budget settling at $4 million, he remembered an offer of help from an unexpected source.

Backtrack to the sultry days of touring film festivals with *Cronos*; sampling life beyond the borders of Mexico for the first time, thinking his moment had come. On one occasion, del Toro was at the Miami Film Festival with Luppi, sipping Diet Coke by a serene pool, when a charming voice called to him in Spanish. 'Are you Guillermo del Toro?'[17]

'And I turned around and it was Pedro Almodóvar!'[18] he recalled, incredulous that he, a nobody, was being approached by Spain's foremost filmmaker, the ebullient, worldly talent behind such bold melodramas as *Law of Desire* and *Tie Me Up! Tie Me Down!*

Following handshakes and unnecessary introductions, Almodóvar mentioned how much he had liked *Cronos*. 'If you ever come to Spain,' he added genuinely, 'my brother and I would like to produce a movie for you.'[19]

Since 1987, Pedro and Augustín Almodóvar had successfully run the production company El Deseo ('The Desire') out of Madrid. Regrettably, del Toro would first be drawn into the clutches of those less convivial brothers, the Weinsteins. It was four years after Almodóvar's casual offer that del Toro took the chance to call him.

'Remember that conversation we had?'[20]

Almodóvar was everything Bob Weinstein was not. His enthusiasm and support ran unabated. He became fascinated with the sheer level of preparation that went into del Toro's filmmaking – he tended to take a more loose-limbed, improvisational approach. When del Toro politely broached the subject of final cut, he was amazed. Why wouldn't he have final cut? He was the director.

The financing would eventually be split between the Almodóvars in Spain and a new production company Alfonso Cuarón had founded with a billionaire partner. How fitting, thought del Toro, that *The Devil's Backbone* could be classified as half-Spanish and half-Mexican.

Significantly, having transplanted his story from Mexico to Spain, he moved his family to California (via Austin), distancing himself from the manifest threats of his homeland. Del Toro has remained Mexican to his core. Every one of his films is in essence a Mexican film. But he lives a self-imposed physical and artistic separation from the land of his birth.

'Every day, every week, something happens that reminds me that I am in involuntary exile,'[21] he reflected sadly.

Dislocation and belonging have become key themes in his work. Subsequent films are populated with outcasts. *The Devil's Backbone* opens with Carlos being delivered to his daunting new home.

Shooting over the summer of 2000 beneath the unforgiving sun of Talamanca, an arid plateau north of Madrid, the production built both the grim exterior and shadowy interiors of the orphanage from scratch. It felt as though they'd been cut off from time. Del Toro had asked Spanish comic-book artist Carlos Giménez to help storyboard the film. Giménez was famed for his autobiographical comic *Paracuellos* (named after a region notorious for Civil War mass killings), which depicted his childhood experiences growing up in brutal state-funded orphanages under the Franco regime. He compared the old, broken buildings to concentration camps.

A huge fan of these tales of boys scuttling through ominous corridors after dark, del Toro wanted to capture something of their complex tone. In a touching subplot, we find that misunderstood bully Jaime (Íñigo Garcés) yearns one day to be a comic-book artist.

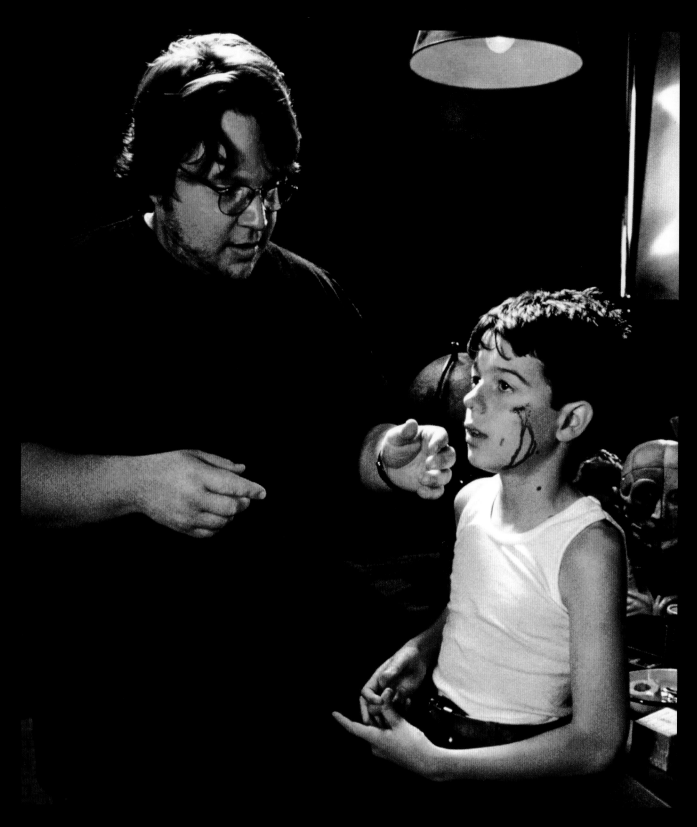

Above: Guillermo del Toro loves to build an air of secrecy, while inserting pivotal action into the background. Here, Conchita (Irene Visedo) goes about her chores, while Dr. Casares (Federico Luppi) and Carmen (Marisa Paredes) confer in the shadows.

Opposite: A gift with children – del Toro's secret is that he treats his child and adult actors just the same, pushing them to draw upon their own memories to create their characters.

Right: Carmen's prosthetic leg, as well as the strange collection of deformed foetuses kept by Dr. Casares, give the film a slight steampunk flavour.

Wisely, del Toro also chose to reunite with cinematographer Guillermo Navarro. They had met many moons before on *Cabeza de Vaca*, a story of conquistadors floundering in sixteenth-century Florida. Del Toro was providing the elaborate native make-up effects, and Navarro could see how inventive – and how ambitious – he was even then.

Navarro had been a temperamental collaborator on *Cronos*, unafraid to speak his mind. He was always searching for something, ready to make everyone's life hell, but always in service of the movie. After *Mimic*, del Toro needed creative unity, and it was as if he and Navarro had already seen it: the desaturated look, like a sepia photograph. Del Toro classified the mood as a genre-blending Western gothic. He wanted earth tones: olives, dusty browns, characters framed in ochre like insects trapped in amber.

'I bust my ass for the movies I do …' he insisted. 'I try to make them gorgeous and I try to make them look big, within their budget, but it's all about communication with the crew. I create these significant memos where I describe the colour palate.'[22]

By night, they shifted from the blaze of a Spaghetti Western into the deep blues of horror, accented with gold, that del Toro had pursued for *Mimic*. How Bob Weinstein would have hated the lyricism of *The Devil's Backbone* – the unhurried pace, the building of mystery, the symbolism, things that go unexplained – but, ironically, del Toro applied the camera style he had learned on *Mimic* to his new film. 'This is a direct result of the studio telling me, "Move the camera around,"'[23] he admitted. A fluid camera becomes a voyeur.

It was an exhausting shoot, but this was a weariness fuelled by ambition, not conflict (plus the pressing matter that the director had already committed to *Blade II*). Del Toro felt the enthralling terror of being answerable only to the movie. 'Alejandro Jodorowsky, the director of *Santa Sangre*, has what he calls the panic method: the man intellectualizes what he's going to do a lot, but then he just goes crazy on it and goes by instinct. It's almost like you're channelling the movie.'[24]

Something unconscious crept into the storytelling: a ghost in the machine. Shooting the climactic sequence with the blast in the kitchen, laying waste to the orphanage – and it was vital to the director's artful scheme that it is *not* the central bomb that explodes, but a leak of kerosene gas – del Toro realized that fate played its part. In the scene in question, Luppi's blood-soaked Casares comes to, his head still spinning, and staggers around assessing the damage. With the evening light fading, del Toro decided to grab it in one handheld shot, as if the camera was dizzy. On their first go, here was the perfect take: the boys were sobbing on cue, and the sun hit the smoke at the ideal ninety degrees. Entirely unforeseen was the fact that by blowing the kitchen doors off a natural vacuum had been created – like a horizontal chimney – and the smoke was moving in and out of the doorway in the back of the shot as if the building was gasping for breath. Years later, del Toro would replicate the effect on *Crimson Peak*. Happenstance became a motif.

Opposite below: A mortally wounded Dr. Casares (Federico Luppi) tries to comfort Jaime (Íñigo Garcés). Guillermo del Toro was thrilled to work again with the Argentine actor, who had done so much for his debut *Cronos*.

Right: The attention of Jaime (Íñigo Garcés) is drawn to the fateful bomb plummeting through the night sky …

Below: … to crash into the courtyard without exploding. For del Toro the metaphorical bomb became the central image – this symbol of unfinished business.

Left: The lost boys – one of the main influences on the film was *Lord of the Flies*, but Guillermo del Toro found hope in the youngsters working together.

Opposite: While it wasn't a great success on its initial release, *The Devil's Backbone* really set the seal on the director's career.

It was on *The Devil's Backbone* that del Toro began his habit of writing miniature bios for each of the main characters: brief surveys from birth to their most recent birthday to help the actors create a life beyond the bounds of the screenplay. The world of the movie needed to feel lived in and worn out.

As with Tamara Shanath in *Cronos*, del Toro's instinct for an eerie form of childhood innocence was unerring. He christened the boys his 'seven dwarves'[25] and knew them immediately. Tielve, his lead, had read for an extra, but he had these big, sad Paul McCartney eyes. Garcés, as Jaime, had the gangling frame of a boy on the cusp of adolescence. He looked as if his bones itched. On set, del Toro treated child and adult actors alike. They needed to identify with their characters. Think of your saddest memory, he instructed. Use it. After all, wasn't he doing the same thing?

In the original Trashorras and Mũnoz screenplay, the story encircled a ghostly caretaker who tended the bomb like a delicate flower. There are early sketches in del Toro's notebooks that presage a desiccated, Lurch-like figure, with a hint of Boris Karloff as Frankenstein's creature.

But, as with the vampire of *Cronos*, del Toro's instinct was to reverse the poles. The ghost must evoke our sympathy in equal proportion to the evil emerging in the beautiful guise of Jacinto. So we get a drowned boy with unfinished business. The look of Santi makes as vivid an impression as Jesús Gris. It was vital he should never resemble a zombie. With that ivory skin, he looks like a porcelain doll. Del Toro wanted the spirituality implicit in the character's name to be manifest in his every sense. He picked Valverde for his angelic looks. Santi's tears leave rusty stains of a weeping statue. Oxide

is everywhere, as if the bomb's surface had spread like an infection into the walls of the orphanage.

They utilized early versions of CGI to give the impression of bones visible beneath the skin. Particle effects caused the air to blur around Santi as if he was still submerged in water, blood permanently blooming like smoke from a gash in his forehead. A similar distorting effect would be used to give scale to the gigantic robots of *Pacific Rim*.

Santi haunts the passageways of the orphanage by night, luring Carlos to the vaulted cellar with its great open cistern. Water takes its place as the primary element of the del Toro universe. This is the scene of his murder, but Santi is not a threat so much as a messenger. He is frightening, to be sure. A harbinger of doom with his head split open like an egg (becoming hardboiled as another del

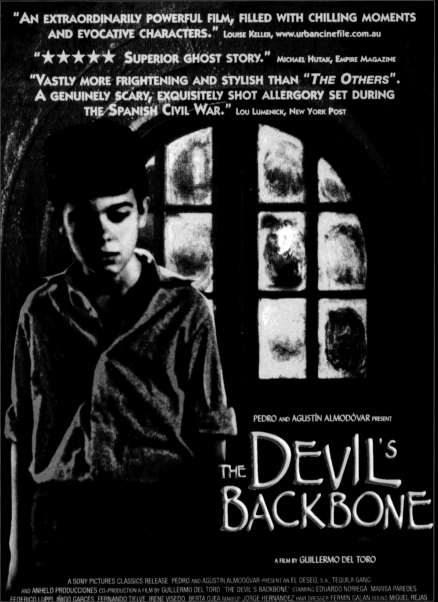

PEDRO AND AGUSTÍN ALMODÓVAR PRESENT

THE DEVIL'S BACKBONE

A FILM BY GUILLERMO DEL TORO

Toro motif). But the director is taking a political stance with the supernatural: 'You should be afraid of the guys who made the ghost.'[26]

Santi is the Republic drowned by the fascists.

'The entire Civil War is a ghost that still haunts Spain,'[27] declared del Toro. He was wrapping the political into the personal.

The true villain, Jacinto, lives with the legacy of a loveless father. Abandoned at the orphanage, he is the embodiment of how fascism had corroded the Spanish soul. So he is cruel but poignant, and wonderfully played by Noriega, who came with the perfect mix of matinée idol looks and dedication to his craft. There is no one lonelier than a person who hates

del Toro told him. He carries a pain as heavy as the gold that will seal his fate, the first in a line of fallen princes that will take us to Michael Shannon's Strickland in The Shape of Water and Bradley Cooper's Carlisle in Nightmare Alley. Evil comes in many guises, laments del Toro again and again, and so often in the form of 'these guys who have a hurting child inside.'[28]

The most heartbreaking element of the story is surely that of Conchita (Irene Visedo), the beautiful kitchen girl who has fallen for Jacinto, hoping her love might change him.

The Devil's Backbone is the sparest of all del Toro's films, but therein lies its rewarding power. The stark, period setting; the distant rumbling of war; the stark violence much closer to home; the use of the supernatural to test his characters: these are all part of what Kevin Thomas in the Los Angeles Times saw as a 'bleak vision, which is so compelling, unpredictable and unique that The Devil's Backbone really works.'[29]

Released in the shadow of 9/11, this compelling, provocative, subtly optimistic ghost story was smothered by a different national tragedy. No one was quite ready for its cathartic darkness. It would end up with a wan $6.5 million worldwide, but like an unexploded bomb, the film now dominates any view of del Toro's career. Here is the bedrock of his philosophy as man and filmmaker. By the end, as rights are wronged, the adults are left divided and perish to become ghosts. The boys survive because they chose to band together.

'If we could only get it into our head that we are all in the same orphanage,' implored del Toro, 'that none of us belongs anywhere else.'[30]

BLOOD RUSH
Blade II (2002)

How he then gleefully confounded expectations by jumping aboard a slick vampire franchise to make his first mainstream hit, proving it was possible to apply a touch of Mexican spice to Hollywood formula

With those baby-blues twinkling from behind his glasses, Guillermo del Toro made it clear that his next film was to be a very different beast from the last. *The Devil's Backbone* had been meditative, allegorical, a film elegantly forged with visual restraint and depth of character. It had been a personal journey, shot in his native language. Critics were referring to it as art. Whereas *Blade II*, the director declared gleefully, 'is just fun and nastiness.'[1] This was the first time he had 'made a perfectly politically incorrect movie.'[2]

Blade II's hyper-gory fusion of the superhero and horror doctrines tends to get a mixed reception among even the most ardent of del Toro fans. Alejandro González Iñárritu, for one, couldn't fathom why his Mexican brother-in-arms had sold his soul to such junk. 'He berated me for over two hours for making *Blade II*,' recalled del Toro fondly. 'I had to pull off of the freeway and park in a parking lot, and I finally said, "Listen, man, I need to have lunch. I apologize for having made *Blade*."'[3]

Yet there is a good argument that this comic-book sequel is the most important film of his career, and certainly another key piece in his crazy quilt of genres. This was the opportunity to prove he could work, and work well, beneath the aegis of Hollywood; the chance to clear his head of *Mimic*; and an opportunity to show there were more ways than one to skin a vampire.

Above: Rush-hour chaos – Wesley Snipes deals underground justice to the Reapers as superheroic vampire hunter Blade.

Opposite: *Blade II* furthered a superhero franchise that pioneered the genre long before it became popular.

Left: Triple threat – star Wesley Snipes, director Guillermo del Toro and writer-producer David S. Goyer enjoy the premiere, after dark naturally.

Opposite: When del Toro first got into comics, his taste orientated to the horror-theme series, an off-centre sensibility he brought to *Blade II.*

Not that del Toro hadn't had his doubts. He had turned it down three times. 'Like St Peter,'[4] he quipped. *Blade* producer Peter Frankfurt, and writer David S. Goyer, whose 13,000-strong collection of comics rivalled del Toro's, were both big fans of *Cronos.* They had made overtures for him to direct the first *Blade,* spotting its correlation with his finely tuned atmospherics, though it never evolved into a firm offer. Now, with the production company New Line Cinema (part of the Warner Bros. extended family) eager to move forward with a sequel, Frankfurt and Goyer returned to their favourite Mexican. And del Toro said no, repeatedly. He had his heart set on *Hellboy* – a comic-book adaptation of a different hue.

So the canny Goyer applied a bit of reverse Hollywood psychology. 'You wanna do *Hellboy*?'[5] he said, setting the snare. 'You think the studio will finance it from seeing *Devil's Backbone* and *Cronos*?' The industry, he

insisted, would see del Toro as the guy dedicated to spare, gothic stories. 'No, no,' protested del Toro as the snare snapped shut, 'I am this crazy freak who loves to do comic-book action.'[6]

Del Toro doesn't have a dark half – he is a dark whole – but away from the critical recognition there is a trashier, B-movie side to his personality. 'There is a part of me that will always be pulp,'[7] he accepted, and *Blade II* was a six-pack-and-pizza kind of movie. With none of the thwarted ambition of *Mimic,* the film you see is the film he set out to make – on behalf of the studio, and on behalf of his teenage self.

Which was what lay at the root of his lively squabble with Iñárritu. 'It appeals to the vilest of human emotions,'[8] his friend had remonstrated. To which del Toro engaged his most angelic smile. 'Dude, it's a *Tom and Jerry* cartoon.'[9]

He took great delight in the through-the-looking-glass contrast between his recent films, where the

R-rated *Blade II* played young and *The Devil's Backbone,* a tale of lost boys, was 'very adult.'[10] Which doesn't mean to say the new film meant any less to him. But the script was a done deal. In fact, *Blade II* is unique in del Toro's filmography as the only picture that he has directed without taking a writing credit. While he would work with Goyer on structuring the $55 million horror, still implanting layers of meaning into its slime-coated walls, del Toro embraced the appeal of lizard-brained splatter.

'If you find it too loud,' he warned prospective viewers, tongue hovering in cheek, 'you're too old.'[11]

Blade is half-vampire, or a Dhampir. He inherited the scourge after his mother was attacked by a vampire during labour, but can still pass as a very cool human being. Not for Blade the bother of removing his shades in order to look through night-vision goggles. As well as the heightened senses gifted to him by

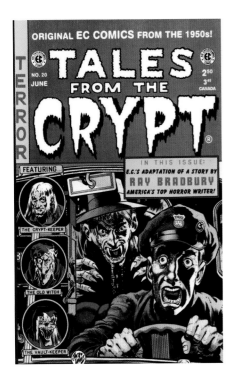

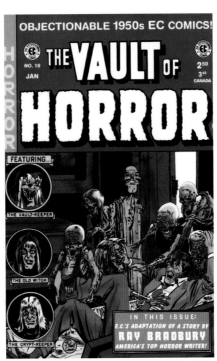

his blood, he is adept at martial arts and immune to daylight. His sworn mission is to exterminate full-blooded vampires, those vile night-crawlers. Rather like in *Mimic*, he is ridding the city of bugs. He is also a rare African-American superhero hailing from the pages of Marvel Comics, who began life, or half-life, in 1973.

Invented by adjacently named writer Marv Wolfman and artist Gene Colan, he took his bow as a supporting hero in *Tomb of Dracula*, sporting a bandolier of blades, motorbike leathers, shades, and an aura of rock star nonchalance. American football star turned 'first black action star'[12] Jim Brown served as a model. Eventually headlining his own run of comics, Blade was both vampire hunter and politically charged messenger for the Civil Rights movement.

Right now, he looked like Wesley Snipes.

When del Toro got into comics, he always veered toward the horror

and mystery titles rather than the mainstream superheroes. Those published beneath gothic banners like *Tales from the Crypt* and *The Vault of Horror*. He liked moral distinctions to be less certain. He liked the monsters. As he had utilized the talents of Carlos Giménez on *The Devil's Backbone*, he sought out *Hellboy* creator Mike Mignola to storyboard *Blade II*, injecting the cellular art form into the film's conceptual roots.

Though they hail from the famous comic-book stable, the *Blade* films predate the all-consuming Marvel Cinematic Universe (with its high-flying *Iron Men* and proliferating *Avengers*) – they are an outlier of the superhero movement, as would be the avant-garde *Hellboy*. The overriding atmosphere is still one of horror.

The plot devised by Goyer has two vampire emissaries of the Bloodpack pay the gloomy hero a surprise visit. The Bloodpack, featuring Ron Perlman's sourpuss Reinhardt among

their number, are a crack team of hipster vampires sworn to kill Blade. In their co-ordinated jet-black couture, combining the fascist with the fetishist (all del Toro-designed), they resemble the disposable squad that might inhabit an *Alien* movie. They have a similar problem. A pandemic is rife among vampires, which transforms them into an extreme mutation known as Reapers. Shorn of all their usual vulnerabilities – to garlic, crosses, stakes etc. – they crave the enriched blood of 'normal' vampires. Keeping his own enigmatic counsel (Blade is unusually aloof among the impassioned characters of the del Toro oeuvre), the vampire hunter will team up with the vampires to track down the Reaper known as Nomak (Luke Goss) – who, as the Patient Zero of the outbreak, carries the secret of its origin. Trust between all parties will remain in a fluid state.

This was an exercise in keeping things simple – not overthinking your strategy, or dwelling on the context. A sequel had to be obedient. 'It was a great exercise to refrain myself from being in the spotlight, while at the same time, putting all my heart into it,'[13] said del Toro.

Given access to every inch of film shot on the original, he made a study of *Blade* take by take. He appreciated how it 'had this fuck-you attitude.'[14] Which was also a concern. Del Toro was conscious he wasn't hip. He hadn't made videos for rap stars. He preferred the dark of cinemas to clubs. All that, New Line reassured him, would be covered off by Snipes; they wanted the uncool cool stuff of which he was proving a master.

As much as he adhered to franchise rules, there are refrains here only del Toro would dare play. He was one of a generation of directors who embraced the staccato light-shows of videogames; as much a child of *Doom* as of Lewis

Carroll, and *Blade II* is infected with the frenetic, forward momentum and maze-like confines of the classic first-person shooter. He claimed that 'videogames are a genuine narrative form.'[15] Furthermore, he can see a point on the horizon when film and game will begin to merge artistically. 'The art direction, soundscapes and immersive environments in videogames are as good, if not superior to, most movies.'[16] The downside is that, if anything, they are even harder to get made.

As of 2019, there exists a litany of attempts to create the signature del Toro videogame. Each was wildly ambitious, with dreams, and availability, often at odds with the reality of building games, which was as painstaking as raising a skyscraper.

Sundown, a failed zombie shooter from 2006, was due to be part of a multi-media franchise that proliferated into film and television. *InSane*, a Lovecraftian work-in-progress cancelled in 2012, was to begin with a detective in search of his lost family, and end with a cosmic monstrosity the size of a mountain. In 2015, del Toro joined forces with Hideo Kojima, the near-mythical developer behind *Metal Gear Solid*. They planned a new entry in the *Silent Hill* series, a world of psychological horror spun around a haunted town. They were equally drawn to 'melancholic ideas,'[17] del Toro told the audience at a game convention in Las Vegas. However, he added, 'the bastards with the money'[18] weren't quite on the same wavelength. The axe fell.

He and Kojima stayed in touch. Indeed, for Kojima's 2019 release, *Death Stranding*, he strapped on a motion-capture suit to have his exact likeness appear within the game as the character of Deadman – an artificial human built from harvested cadavers like 'Frankenstein's monster.'[19]

This was all to come, of course. For the time being, with *Blade II*, he was attempting a synthesis of the comic-book and videogame aesthetic on film – as well as drawing upon his love of anime, the exotic brand of Japanese animation that sprang out of the teeming sagas of the famed manga comics. During the shoot, he would slip Snipes DVDs – *Ninja Scroll* and the cyberpunk duo of *Ghost in the Shell* and *Akira* – to give him a foretaste of his elaborate schemes.

Right: Martial arts superstar Donnie Yen served as both star (in the guise of Snowman) and fight choreographer, imbuing the action with the exoticism of Eastern cinema.

Opposite: Enemies united – Bloodpack leader Nyssa (Leonor Varela) strikes a deal with mortal enemy Blade (Wesley Snipes), as gadget guru Scud (Norman Reedus) keeps a sceptical distance.

Below: Suited and booted, a team shot of the Bloodpack. *From left:* Chupa (Matt Schulze), Nyssa (Varela), Asad (*Red Dwarf's* Danny John-Jules), Verlaine (Marit Velle Kile), Reinhardt (*Cronos'* Ron Perlman), and Snowman (Yen).

In 2001, Snipes was at the height of his box office appeal. Having worked across the spectrum from relationship dramas (*Jungle Fever, One Night Stand*) and high-energy comedies (*White Men Can't Jump*) to hip-hop crime thrillers (*New Jack City*), he was now – for good and ill – transformed into a major action star by *Blade*. By the third in the trilogy, the inferior *Blade Trinity*, his salary was $13m. The brooding, Florida-born star was also executive producer, a fifth dan in Shotokan karate, and notoriously difficult to deal with.

Wise to Hollywood's emotional foibles, del Toro put a deal to his leading man. If you look after Blade, he promised, 'I'll make you look good and handle everything else.'[20] Aside from a couple of minor disagreements, Snipes did his thing, landing the fight scenes without ruffling the character's perpetual sangfroid.

'Blade is a character that doesn't change,' shrugged del Toro, 'that's part of the joy – he's not reading T.S. Eliot and crying by the end.'[21]

Shooting from March to July, 2001, based out of the Barrandov Studios in the fairy-tale city of Prague, del Toro set about making what was at once his most futuristic (until *Pacific Rim*) and still richly gothic story thus far. The vampires might be armed to their pointy teeth with cutting-edge weaponry, but they skirt the sunlight by roaming an ancient sewer system.

As a boy, the intrepid del Toro explored Guadalajara's sewers on foot. They were like another world. A sewer, he perceived, is a labyrinth that runs beneath the surface, a way of passing unseen, and a visual metaphor for the passageways of plot. Writers as diverse as Stephen King (*It*) and Victor Hugo (*Les Misérables*) have explored the narrative possibilities of such

subterranean channels. The *Teenage Mutant Ninja Turtles* lived in the New York sewers, as did the mutant insects of *Mimic*.

What you didn't tend to see or read about, noted del Toro, were the vast stalactites of white mucus, basically these huge, pendulous bacterial cultures. Scouting the Prague sewers for *Blade II*, surprised at how little this brick underworld had been utilized by filmmakers, he found alcoves full of the same mucus, giving off the same whiff of old yogurt. He was in his element. These damp passages will lead Blade and what's left of the Bloodpack to the villain's hi-tech lair. Shot in virtual monochrome, it is like watching vampires swarming through the same shimmering tunnels where Harry Lime meets his fate in *The Third Man*.

Above: Gravity-defying Reapers close in on Wesley Snipes' Blade – the icy-blue look of the brickwork tunnel and the exaggerated shadows are pure Guillermo del Toro.

Opposite: The ice-cool hero poses, unusually, without sunglasses. Well aware Snipes had a reputation for being difficult, del Toro would leave the star to look after Blade, while he got on with depicting the vampires.

Right: Snipes in mid-flow, emphasizing the sequel's athletic blurring of genres: horror, superhero, action movie with a sideline in martial arts moves, and in its own way, the musical.

The antique catacombs will give way to crackpot futuristic concoctions made of giant steel pipes like a chocolate factory of the undead. Del Toro liked to think of the sequel as a pseudo-Bond movie: unchangeable hero and megalomaniac baddie clash in a giant Ken Adam-style set. Blade also has his share of gadgets – boomerang blades, skin-cleaving bombs, and UV grenades – provisioned by Norman Reedus as geeky sidekick Scud, but hatched in the director's notebooks.

Like its predecessor, the sequel leans into the martial arts arena. Chinese star Donnie Yen, a veteran of the Hong Kong (China) movie scene, plays the sleek, silent Snowman as well as choreographing the fight scenes to his contemporary brand of balletic violence. To learn his chops, del Toro immersed himself in the cream of Hong Kong (China) cinema, such as Yen's performance in *Iron Monkey*, catching its heightened reality in his hyperkinetic camera moves.

He wanted the action heightened to the point it was 'almost a musical of violence.'[22] So he was blasting away vampires in cascades of blood, scorching them to ashes in shards of daylight, mixing CGI with physical effects, while channelling the effervescence of *West Side Story*.

The most vivid expression of this mad duality is in The House of Pain, a vampire nightclub that lives up to its billing as the camera roves through a menu of graphic S&M (unzippable spinal cords, anyone?) Soaked in strobes and hot neon, the whole underground scene has the essence of a debauched *Blade Runner*. Mid-rave, the Bloodpack take on an outrider of Reapers, a battle del Toro orchestrates as a series of individual duals within the tribal frenzy of the dance. It's a virtuoso piece of editing,

and possibly the freakiest thing he has ever done.

'I just loved all the gore,'[23] he enthused. As far as he was concerned, this wasn't real violence. Certainly compared to the sharp stabs of barbarity in *The Devil's Backbone*. 'It's exploitation,'[24] he said.

Quite apart from any wider career objectives, del Toro agreed to direct *Blade II* on the condition that he could design the Reapers to his liking. 'Then I got excited,'[25] he said. He was back in the laboratory creating monsters. In this case, a vampire unlike anything we had ever seen, yet one that still paid homage to the bloodsucking traditions of film and literature. This was where he could truly impose himself on the sequel.

Back in that inquisitive Mexican childhood, greedy for detail, del Toro fed on vampire movies, vampire comics, and all the vampire classics from Bram Stoker to Anne Rice. Going deeper still, he filled his head with legends and folktales. He knew how the concept of the vampire differed between countries. Such knowledge had fuelled the early subversions of *Cronos*, transforming the suave complexion of Dracula into an eccentric old man slipping into addiction. He began to conceive of a biological reality for vampirism, injecting his action movie with metaphors for the AIDS crisis that infiltrated the club scene.

Left: A double-crossing Nyssa flees Blade – shot in the Prague sewers, the light reflecting off the brickwork deliberately references the underground chase sequence at the end of *The Third Man*.

Left: Richard Sammel leads a gang of the infected in *The Strain* – while not directly related, Guillermo del Toro's 2014 television series, based on his own novel, continues the themes (vampirism as disease) and look of *Blade II*.

Opposite above: Kris Kristofferson returns as Whistler, mentor to Blade – father figures would reoccur in many of del Toro's films.

Opposite below: Meanwhile, vampire king Damaskinos (Thomas Kretschmann) is another corrupt mastermind on a quest for immortality.

The centuries-old tradition of creating fictional monsters has been a way of examining our own frailties through a ritualization of deformity and disease. There is a 1751 treatise, a genuine del Toro favourite entitled *Dissertations Upon the Apparitions of Angels, Daemons, and Ghosts, and Concerning Vampires of Hungary, Bohemia, Moravia, and Silesia*, which established that vampirism is a contagion. The Romanian concept of the *Strigoi*, undead spirits revitalized by blood, drew upon the concept of blood parasites.

'The vampires came from me figuring out vampirism for *Cronos*,'[26] he explained, but he was moving in very different direction. They were to be, he relished, 'a much more animalistic vampire.'[27]

Del Toro returned to a series of sketches he had made for *I Am Legend*. Still young, with *Cronos* his only credit, he had been asked to pitch for the huge Warner Bros. adaptation, due to star Arnold Schwarzenegger as the last man alive. A fan of Richard Matheson's post-apocalyptic novel, he

had delivered intricate concepts for humanity's devolution into vampiric beasts. However, he recalled ruefully, this 'twenty-eight-year-old twerp from Mexico' then made it clear that 'Arnold'[28] in no way stood as the representative of common man. Warner didn't call back.

A good monster, del Toro can assure anyone, should be unveiled in a series of surprises like layers to be unpeeled.

The outermost layer of the Reapers mixes his *I Am Legend* prototypes with the classic rendition of the vampire seen in *Nosferatu* and the 1979 television version of Stephen King's *Salem's Lot*: hairless, a delta of veins beneath sallow skin, and bloodshot eyes with white irises. Then the Reaper's lower jaw cracks open and unfurls into a great fanged orifice. Any likeness to *Predator* is purely intentional. From within, an *Alien*-like extendible tongue, with its own set of fangs and micro-tentacles, latches onto a victim.

'The Reapers are the masterpieces of this movie,'[29] wrote critic Roger Ebert, delighting in their tripartite

snouts. But it doesn't stop there. Del Toro's brew of science and the supernatural goes full autopsy. After the comic mortician sequence in *Cronos*, insect vivisection in *Mimic*, and Dr. Casares's foetal dabblings in *The Devil's Backbone*, the post-mortem has become a del Toro ritual or in-joke wherein the various design stages of monster physiognomy get re-enacted.

The basis for Reaper biology touches on theories he came up with for *Cronos*, but could never afford. Ideas that would come to fruition in *The Strain*, the 2014 vampire outbreak series based on novels del Toro co-wrote with Chuck Hogan. The Reaper's heart comes encased in bone. So stakes are of no use. There are 'bifurcated masseter muscles'[30] for a stronger bite, while neurotoxins are released by stinger-like teeth, paralyzing the victim. When it came to sucking blood, del Toro coolly noted, it was like finding a leech in your armpit. The Reaper metabolism, we learn, is so fast it will burn out in twelve hours unless the creatures feed, but it has made them as agile

and strong as panthers. It's this kind of gruesome intricacy that elevates *Blade II* above its franchise. A movie 'steamed in the dread cauldrons of the filmmaker's imagination,'[31] Ebert went on to say, waxing diabolical.

At the centre of the maze is the vampire king Eli Damaskinos, played by the charming German actor Thomas Kretschmann (*Stalingrad, U-571*) beneath ghoulish prosthetics, evidently primeval in age. Damaskinos, it turns out, is a vampiric Dr. Frankenstein yearning to purify his race by weaning out its genetic frailties. QED: the Reapers. But his guinea-pig son has turned on his father. And it is in Goss's desperate Nomak that the film finds its drama. Del Toro's artful pendulum

Right: A display of Reaper sculptures from Guillermo del Toro's *At Home with My Monsters* exhibition in 2019. The chance to design the Reapers' extraordinary physiognomy was one the chief reasons he took on the sequel.

Left: Luke Goss, as the tragic central Reaper Nomak, poses with a delighted director. While others mocked del Toro for taking on a lurid studio film, he remains unrepentant. Indeed, he considers *Blade II* as much a personal film as the likes of *Pan's Labyrinth*.

Opposite: Feast your eyes on the foyer of Bleak House, del Toro's personal mansion of wonders. Other than the looming face of Boris Karloff as Frankenstein's creature, you can spot a statue of a Sammael creature from *Hellboy*, and on the left wall Viktor Safonkin's *St. George and the Dragon*, which would have been inspiration for the look of Smaug in his version of *The Hobbit*.

swings from action into 'a dynastic tragedy about the bonds and rivalries of fathers and their sons.'[32] You can feel his hand take the tiller of the storytelling. Here too is a monarch's fear of ageing – that same idea of immortality as curse and addiction that hangs over from *Cronos*.

Beneath the hyperbolic violence swam what *Slant Magazine* called his 'spiritual, entomological freaky-deakyness.'[33]

Remarkably, as the shoot progressed, New Line had virtually left del Toro alone. They had their hands full with *The Lord Of The Rings*, he surmised, which proved a useful distraction. On seeing the finished film, they were shocked into silence, but didn't touch a thing. Before them was a blend of art and pulp, and their

nervy faith was justified with an opening weekend blast of $32 million. The film would go on to make $82m in the USA, and $155 worldwide, outgunning the original.

'*Blade II*,' acknowledged del Toro, 'was priceless in my life.'[34] It accelerated the metabolism of his career, securing him a Hollywood berth, as he moved from Austin to Los Angeles, setting up home in the San Fernando Valley, a safe distance from the pretensions of Beverly Hills. Three minutes away in Westlake Village, success allowed him to buy another mansion to serve as a reliquary for his collection, which he gave the Dickensian designation of Bleak House.

Mock Tudor by design, with tinted windows and a weathervane in the

sinewy shape of a dragon, del Toro joked that this was a 'man-cave of epic proportions.'[35] In grander terms, it is what medieval Germans might have referred to as a *wunderkammer* – a 'wonder room' in which wealthy nobles housed their bizarre and fabulous relics.

Bleak House represents almost everything del Toro has amassed since childhood, a vast Smaugian hoard that has travelled with him into exile. 'Every book I have ever read and most every toy I ever bought,'[36] he confirmed proudly, taking his cue from a visit to science-fiction doyen Ray Bradbury's house in Cheviot Hills, abundant with keepsakes. 'Never throw out anything you love,'[37] he had admonished this young Mexican acolyte.

'As a kid, I dreamed of having a house with secret passages and a room where it rained twenty-four hours a day,' he recounted. 'The point of being over forty is to fulfil the desires you've been harbouring since you were seven.'[38]

Bleak House is a kingdom of rooms subdivided by theme and purpose. In the foyer you will find *St. George and the Dragon*, a painting by Russian artist Viktor Safonkin which hints at where del Toro might have gone with Smaug if he had made *The Hobbit*, while an enormous head of Boris Karloff as Frankenstein's creature stares from the gallery above. The wooden floors are polished to the mirrored sheen of a Regency ballroom. The walls are deep crimson. You are instantly reminded of films: teeming Xanadu from *Citizen Kane*, J.F. Sebastian's apartment cluttered with his oddball toys in *Blade Runner*, and the Escher-like passages of the monastery in *The Name of the Rose*.

It is a geek's dream, an artist's stronghold. Every room is curated like a personal museum. Dating back to before *Cronos*, here are all the storyboards, scripts, models and maquettes from his movies, testament to his devotion to physical filmmaking. When he isn't lost to a film production, he comes here for at least two hours every day, like chapel.

Downstairs, the Horror Library harbours taxonomized volumes on vampires, factual and fictional. There are also several puppets of Nosferatu, and a full-sized sculpture of H.P. Lovecraft. 'As far as good horror,' reported del Toro, listing off favourites as his eyes roamed shelf after alphabetized shelf, 'well, anything by Ramsey Campbell, Algernon Blackwood, Arthur Machen, Joseph Sheridan Le Fanu, M.R. James, Stephen

King, William Hope Hodgson, Lovecraft, Robert W. Chambers.'[39]

The Comic Book Library houses his drafting table. There is also the Sun Room, the Manga Room, the Screening Room (where a bronze mask of Hitchcock peers haughtily from the wall), the Steampunk Room, and the Studio (where invited concept artists work during the early stages of his movies). There is even an overflow mansion a block away.

A secret door hidden behind a bookcase (naturally) leads to his inner sanctum. With its fireplace, soft leather sofa, and large oak desk, it has the antique mood of a garret belonging to one of his great forebears. A Poe or a

Above: A stunning carving of the Angel of Death from *Hellboy II: The Golden Army* preserved at Bleak House. The Angel was a visual expansion of the Pale Man in *Pan's Labyrinth* with his eyes found at the folds of his wings.

Opposite: The Horror Library features this imposingly lifelike statue of H.P. Lovecraft rudely interrupted from his book. The award-wining American sculptor Thomas Kuebler did all the full-sized silicone character studies at Bleak House.

Dickens, a Machen or a James could be pictured here, summoning worlds on paper. False windows peer onto darkness until, at the flick of a switch, lightning flashes, thunderclaps ring out, and rain lashes the glass with the meteorological gusto of *Wuthering Heights*. The boy from Mexico can command the weather. It is known as the Rain Room.

This is where he writes his scripts, sealed in a gothic womb beside the statue of Boris Karloff being made up as *Frankenstein's* creature. On the wall is a painting of del Toro's hometown of Guadalajara, in which the artist has captured 'exactly how the light falls in the afternoon...'[40]

Bleak House is more than a collection. This is the nearest we come to peering inside del Toro's head. In his novel *Dreamcatcher* (and the flawed 2003 adaptation), Stephen King portrayed a man trapped inside his own memory – visualized as a vast dusty storeroom filled with box files. With the distinctly more refined air of a classy *fin-de-siècle* hotel, these are the quiet halls of del Toro's imagination, the immaculate warehouse of all that has inspired and goes on inspiring him.

'You're God as an artist,' he proposed, 'and it's really just the way you arrange. I think a director is an arranger. I direct this house, and everything goes somewhere, and I can tell you why, and there are thematic pairings, or there is a wall with all blue on it. There is nothing accidental. And my movies are like my house.'[41]

Bleak House is a retreat, a sanctuary, a place to recharge his creative batteries, and a work of del Toro art. Surrounded by the thousandfold eyes of his gods, it is here he dreams up new monsters.

Halfway up the stairs, in the company of a life-sized figure of Pinhead from Tod Browning's *Freaks*

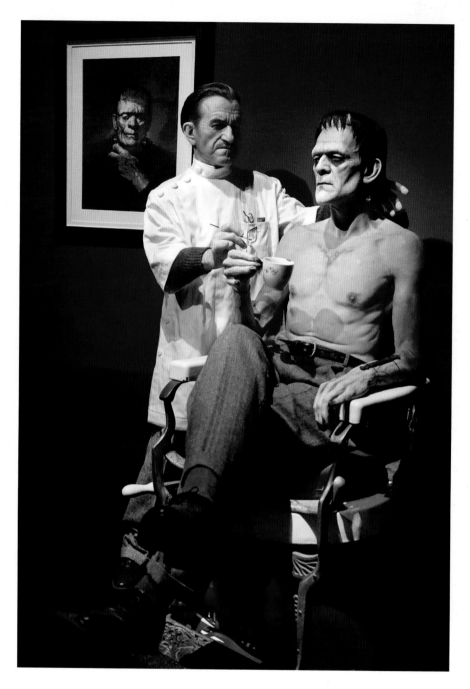

and original H.R. Giger artwork, can be found a range of busts, figurines and maquettes notable for being the colour of ketchup. In various heroic poses, this is the great demon Anung Un Rama, better known as *Hellboy*...fictionally speaking del Toro's best friend.

Above: Found within the inner sanctum of Bleak House, the Rain Room, this silicone statue shows Jack Pierce making up Boris Karloff as the iconic creature in *Frankenstein*.

The Three Amigos

Fellow Mexicans, directors, and best friends, Guillermo del Toro, Alfonso Cuarón, and Alejandro González Iñárritu speak the same language

Left: The magnificent Mexicans: Alejandro González Iñárritu, Guillermo del Toro and Alfonso Cuarón.

It is somehow a comfort to know that Mexico's most celebrated filmmakers are not rivals but firm friends and frequent collaborators. Almost as one, del Toro, Cuarón, and Iñárritu rose out of the independent scene in their homeland to make good on the world stage as three of the most daring and innovative filmmakers at large, regardless of nationality. But they have never forsaken their Mexican identity. It is the essential ingredient to their success and friendship.

'Our generation came out of a brutal moment in the eighties where Mexican cinema was being suffocated,'[1] recalled del Toro. The Mexican government, he explained, was basically against the idea of a Mexican cinema. So they were forced to make their way in independent productions, working for older directors. As their paths inevitably crossed, each knew what it was to struggle, and to burn with ambition.

'We were all trying to do different types of art,' said del Toro. 'Then something happened. The unions opened up and we could make cinema at a professional level and we took it and ran with it.'[2]

They were christened The Three Amigos in jest (after the loco Steve Martin comedy). But given there is now an academic study entitled *The three amigos: The transnational filmmaking of Guillermo del Toro, Alejandro González Iñárritu and Alfonso Cuarón*, that now

counts as an official designation. Their styles are markedly different and yet intimately connected.

Iñárritu spent a wild youth travelling the world before a brief period as a rock radio host. From there, he worked his way up from composer to screenwriter to directing commercials. He broke through with the mesmerizing portmanteau Mexico City comedy-thriller *Amores Perros*, likened to the narrative games of Quentin Tarantino. He mixes a grittier, philosophical side, often built around intersecting stories (*21 Grams*, *Babel*), with a taste for the surreal and epic more akin to del Toro: *Birdman or (The Unexpected Virtue of Ignorance)* and *The Revenant*.

Cuarón, the eldest, floats a little closer to del Toro in style. He worked as a technician in television, likewise baptised by genre in *The Twilight Zone*-esque series *La Hora Marcada* (which Cuarón dubbed 'The Toilet Zone'[3]), before breaking into Hollywood with literary adaptations of *A Little Princess* and *Great Expectations*. He has

brought a tangy realism to genre titles like *Children of Men*, *Harry Potter and the Prisoner of Azkaban*, and *Gravity*. Mixing his mainstream work with highly personal projects rooted in the Mexico of his youth: *Y tu mamá también* and *Roma*.

In an industry of sharks and vipers, each of the Amigos has become dependent on the others' opinion. They have served as producers and advisors on fellow projects, spending time in each other's editing rooms – where they can be relied on to be brutally honest.

Del Toro laughed. 'We have discussions and say, "This shot, this shot, and that shot have to go." And somebody always says, 'But that's a hundred-thousand-dollar shot, plus all the VFX and the set construction ...' It doesn't matter. No one [watching the movie] knows what went on behind the scenes, artistically or economically.'[4]

Together they make their individual films better. To start a Mexican Wave you have to be in sync.

BIG RED

Hellboy (2004) & Hellboy II: The Golden Army (2008)

How he adapted his favourite comic book into a cult superhero film
that combined action, horror, and vivid, steampunk designs, with a
sardonic leading man the colour of lipstick. And a sequel that was
even more elaborate

Before plunging into the bold,
badass world of *Hellboy* and
its bolder and extra badass sequel,
we should briefly shine a light on a
necessary part of Guillermo del Toro's
creative process that goes all the way
back to *Cronos*. Something so natural
you could call it an instinct.

Basically, before production he
will spend months establishing a
particular metaphorical ambience for
his storytelling. Think of it as setting
the table before the banquet is served.
Beginning between the covers of his
notebooks, he consciously invests his
films with meaning. If you linger
over an image, perceiving something
deeper – the fact, say, that the tunnels
in *Pan's Labyrinth* resemble female
apertures, or that the curling horns
on the Faun echo the shape of ovaries
– then you can be certain del Toro
planned it that way.

It is in these formative stages that
he plants those 'visual rhymes'[1] that
cross between films: bottled foetuses,
bloodshot eyeballs or bone-white skin
for instance. He calls them 'fetishes.'[2]

As with the mothership of Bleak
House, he sees his films as rooms
interconnected by theme, design and
subconscious magic. He hasn't made
twelve different movies so much as
'a single movie made of all those
movies.'[3] And those still to be made.
Each feeds into the others, not as a
single cinematic universe like Marvel,
but in a multiverse of worlds between
which del Toro can travel at whim.

Above: Ron Perlman's
Hellboy in his natural habitat
– the comic books presented
Guillermo del Toro with an
enticing hybrid of action
movie and gothic horror.

Opposite: Hellboy's
costume was elaborated to
fit Perlman's personality –
including the striking Civil
War duster coat.

'I believe form is content,' he insisted. 'It's impossible to conceive a movie without first conceiving it in the texture of colour, shape, sets.'[4] With Kubrickian zeal, del Toro determines every facet that goes before his camera, be it a button, the cut of a suit, or a set as vaulted as a cathedral.

Eye candy, he likes to say, is for Hollywood. He does 'eye protein.'[5]

Hellboy was going to be eye protein on steroids. It was based on the cult comic-book series by Californian-born artist and writer Mike Mignola, which had been a wild hit for del Toro's addiction to monsters. From the moment he picked up an issue, he had been 'desperately in love,'[6] and he was a high-level comic-book geek with exacting standards. For the record, other favourites faithfully listed include: *Domu, Coffin, The Sandman, Watchmen, The Killing Joke,* and *Batman Year One.*

First published in 1993, *Hellboy* plays like a caffeinated variation on the del Toro aesthetic: occult paraphernalia, Gothic interiors, arcane rituals, clockwork Nazi assassins, a cornucopia of monsters, and a twisted sense of humour provided by its hardboiled antihero – a six foot six, Ferrari-red demon trying to do the right thing by ridding the world of less reformed demons and assorted associates. He's known as Hellboy; but friends call him Red.

'Mignola has created a unique blend of pulp, horror, [Josh] Kirby dynamics and blue-collar attitude that makes it just impossible to resist,'[7] rejoiced del Toro. One of the few things that got him through the dark nights of *Mimic* was the thought of the next issue coming out, and with it the glimmer of a future adaptation.

The secret to Hellboy, for del Toro, was his fallibility. 'He is like a monument to human vulnerability,' he

extolled. 'He has the extraordinary job of hunting down monsters, but he goes at it like a blue-collar plumber.'[8]

He was never going to make a movie about some lean, good-looking superhero with a chiselled grin. He needed to identify with his leading man. 'I am Hellboy!'[9] he declared, and with great power comes great pettiness. Given the chance, del Toro knew he too would use his abilities to steal a beer, or throw a rock at a guy trying to move in on his girlfriend. The central theme of his screenplay is recognizing that we all have darkness in our nature. Which goes entirely anticlockwise to standard Hollywood thinking, where heroes locate their inner decency.

HELLBOY
TUNNEL "A" / CHAMBER
Bridge leading to Kroenen's Room

MIGNOLA
8/24

Above: *Hellboy's* creator Mike Mignola provided artwork and storyboards for the film, helping to conjoin his distinctive style with that of the director.

Left: Case in point – the labyrinthine underworld of Rasputin's mausoleum with its vast clockwork paraphernalia. Notice too how strikingly the scarlet Hellboy stands out from the background.

Hellboy is a story of nature versus nurture. He is another of del Toro's characters defined by their choices, not their origins. He may have been born in Hell, but under the indulgent tutelage of his adopted father, the kindly paranormal expert Professor 'Broom' Bruttenholm (John Hurt), Hellboy will develop a lopsided moral code, symbolically filing away his great horns. When the mad Russian monk Grigori Rasputin (Karel Roden) is resurrected, intent on enrolling Hellboy into cosmic wickedness, it becomes the story of two fathers batting for the soul of their son.

'I was coming out of my father being kidnapped in Mexico in 1997,' recalled del Toro, 'and I was incredibly invested in the little fable of what it is to be a father and what it is to be a son.'[10]

For all the *monstruo a monstruo* mayhem that will spill through and beneath the streets of New York and Moscow, it was also to be a romance. The somewhat rocky wooing of the pyrokinetic Liz Sherman (Selma Blair) by a smitten Hellboy is modelled entirely on del Toro's courtship of his then wife of twenty years, Lorenza. Mignola noted that del Toro would be deviating from the comic in having the sixty-year-old protagonist mooning over the girl like a 'lovesick teenager.'[11]

This is at once a superhero film, a romance, a fairy tale, and a film noir.

Opposite: Hellboy (Ron Perlman) consoles his pyrotechnic sweetheart Liz (Selma Blair) – on one level, del Toro saw his adaptation as a romance.

Below: As a devoted fan of the comics, there was no way Guillermo del Toro wasn't going to include Hellboy's iconic, heavyweight revolver known as The Good Samaritan.

In order to break the ice at his first meeting with Mignola, del Toro suggested they immediately announce their ideal candidate to play the postmodern crusader. As one, they both shouted 'Ron Perlman.'[12] That was when del Toro knew they were on the same wavelength. Actor and demon had so much in common: always the biggest man in the room; a grin that can be read a thousand ways; the sense of humour as dry as a martini. 'And that fucking voice,'[13] added del Toro. With that settled, he proclaimed, straight-faced, that he wanted his adaptation 'to be *The Last Emperor* of cheesy comic-book movies.'[14]

As perfect as it all sounded, it took six years for *Hellboy* to be born. A stark lesson del Toro was learning again and again was that the projects you cared about most were the hardest to get made. You needed to be obsessed simply to stay the course.

The battle to make *his* version of *Hellboy* began in 1996 with a meeting with producers Larry Gordon and Lloyd Levin, who had already picked up the rights. *Hellboy The Movie*, as it was, had been spinning wheels at Universal as executives prevaricated. The superhero boom had yet to take flight, and unless the central character (or 'property' in studio talk) had sufficiently universal cachet – a *Superman, Batman,* or *Spider-man* – then they struggled to be taken seriously.

'The first *Hellboy* movie was developed before even *X-Men* was on film,'[15] recalled del Toro. It was a countercultural proposition. Then came the first *Blade*, and the cracks began to appear in the cultural dam. That film, he recognized, was 'instrumental in showing how superhero movies could exist at the end of the twentieth century.'[16] In subtle ways, *Blade* paved the way for *The Matrix* to explode into the world. And then *X-men* scorched prescribed notions of superheroes.

Hellboy was also aided by a change of studio. With Universal still threatening a state of eternal limbo, Columbia (through production company Revolution) stepped in to offer $66 million to make a film that, they hoped, would fit right into the post-*Blade*, post-*Matrix*, post-*X-men* cinematic landscape, where no one quite knew the rules of the game.

Del Toro immediately decamped to a Holiday Inn in northeastern Mexico to work on the script. 'I went through the comics and filled them with highlighter marks and Post-it notes, etc., and then made an inventory in my diary, filled it with images and sketches and then started "living" with my diary and eventually just felt the script was mature enough.'[17]

It was like painting a portrait.

Still, the idea that it looked like Perlman made the studio blanch. As far as they were concerned he was a television star at best. How about The Rock? Or Vin Diesel? Throughout pre-production, del Toro would have to deflect 'suggestions'[18] from misguided studio wonks, who clearly hadn't gotten as far as actually reading the comics. How about Hellboy is a normal teenager, they spit-balled, but when he whispers a magic word he turns into the red giant? How about we make him flesh-toned rather than bright red? How about we give him a Hellboy-cycle? Toy sales were never far from their thoughts. He should have a pet Helldog. Knowing how church folk get, how about we just call him Heckboy?

Del Toro ducked and dived between such misbegotten blue-sky thinking, and kept his eyes firmly on his red prize.

What he had in mind was a mix of origin story and police procedural. We begin, in 1944, with the Nazis turning to occult forces in order to stave off defeat. But the attempts by resurrected recruit Rasputin to open up a gateway to Hell are forestalled by the intervention of Bruttenholm and a plucky squad of US troops. Nevertheless, the door was ajar long enough for an infant demon with baby horns and a large stone fist to scurry through. The latest in del Toro's elaborate prologues would take two weeks to film.

Above: The extraordinary clockwork assassin Karl Ruprecht Kroenen (Czech dancer Ladislav Beran) represents the provocative mix of iconography in *Hellboy* from the occult to Nazi Germany.

Left: Abe Sapien, the mild-mannered merman, was performed by del Toro favourite Doug Jones and given eloquent voice by David Hyde Pierce.

1997
Mimic *(feature film)*
Director, writer

2001

The Devil's Backbone *(feature film)*
Director, writer, executive producer

2002
Blade II *(feature film)*
Director

2004
Hellboy *(feature film)*
Director, writer, fight choreographer

2006
Pan's Labyrinth *(feature film)*
Director, producer, writer

2007
The Orphanage
(feature film)
Executive producer

2008

Hellboy II: The Golden Army *(feature film)*
Director, writer, creature vocals (uncredited)

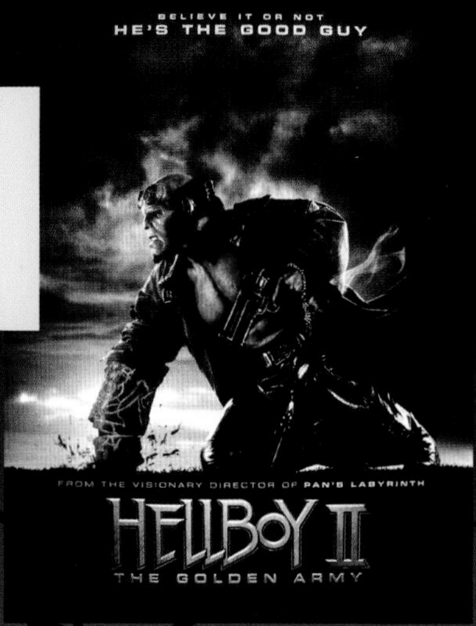

BELIEVE IT OR NOT
HE'S THE GOOD GUY

FROM THE VISIONARY DIRECTOR OF **PAN'S LABYRINTH**

HELLBOY II
THE GOLDEN ARMY

2009

Splice *(feature film)*
Executive producer

"MOST ORIGINAL AND UNIQUE MOVIES OF THE YEAR"

SHE IS NOT
SUPPOSED TO EXIST

A VINCENZO NATALI FILM
ADRIEN BRODY   SARAH POLLEY   DELPHINE CHANEAC

S P L I C E

2011

Kung Fu Panda 2
(animated feature film)
Creative consultant

GUILLERMO
DEL TORO
PRESENTS **DON'T
BE AFRAID OF
THE DARK**

2010

Megamind
(animated feature film)
Creative consultant

2011

Puss in Boots
(animated feature film)
Executive producer,
Moustache man/
Comandante (voices)

2010

Don't Be Afraid of the Dark
(feature film)
Producer, writer

FEAR IS NEVER
JUST MAKE BELIEVE

THE GUILLERMO DEL TORONOMICON

A chronology of the many films and television series that have been touched by the powers of the Mexican magician

1984

El corazón de la noche *(feature film)*
Production assistant (uncredited)

1988-1990

La Hora Marcada *(television series)*
Director, writer, special make-up effects

1986

Doña Lupe *(short film)*
Director, assistant editor, executive producer

1987

Geometria *(short film)*
Director, producer, writer

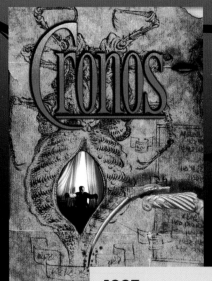

1993

Cronos *(feature film)*
Director, writer

2016-2018

Trollhunters: Tales of Arcadia
(animated television series)
Director, executive producer, writer

2017

The Shape of Water *(feature film)*
Director, producer, writer

2018

Pacific Rim: Uprising
(feature film)
Producer

2018-2019

3Below: Tales of Arcadia
(animated television series)
Director, executive producer,
writer

2019

Scary Stories to Tell in the Dark *(feature film)*
Producer, writer

2020

Wizards: Tales of Arcadia
(animated television series)
Executive producer, writer

2014

The Book of Life (animated feature film)
Producer, Land of the Remembered
Captain's Wife (voice)

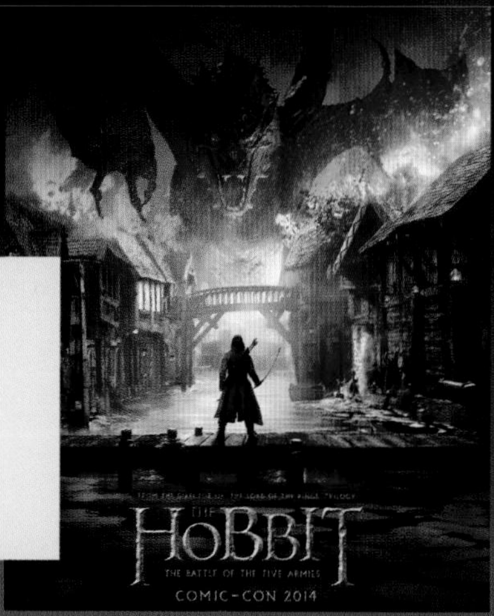

2014

The Hobbit: The Battle of the Five Armies
(feature film)
Writer

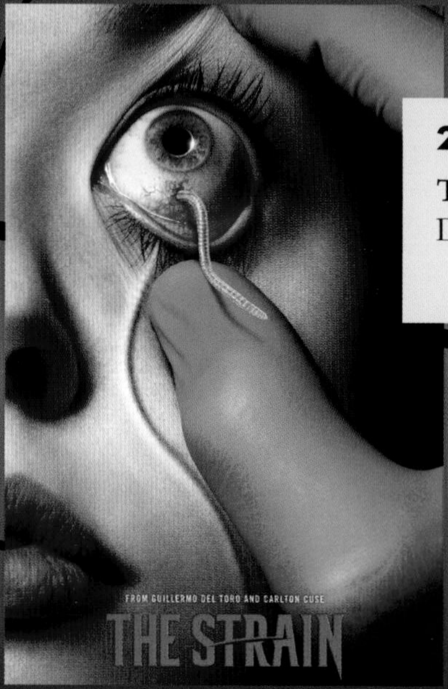

2014-2017

The Strain (television series)
Director, executive producer, writer

2015

Crimson Peak (feature film)
Director, producer, writer

2016

Kung Fu Panda 3
(animated feature film)
Executive producer

2012

Rise of the Guardians
(animated feature film)
Executive producer

2013

Pacific Rim *(feature film)*
Director, producer, writer

2012

The Hobbit: An Unexpected Journey *(feature film)*
Writer

2013

The Hobbit: The Desolation of Smaug *(feature film)*
Writer

2013

Mama *(feature film)*
Executive producer

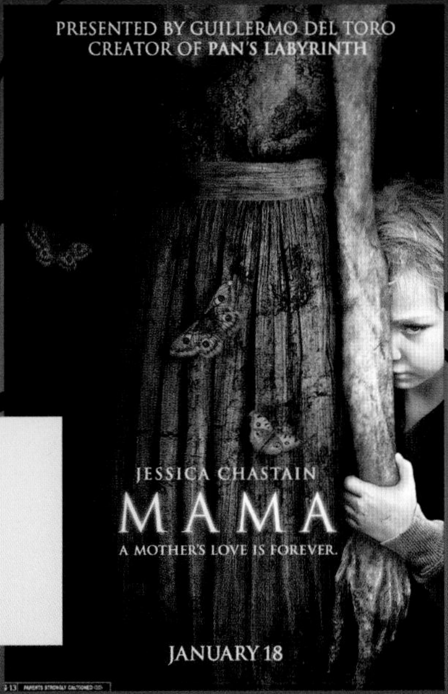

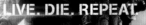

2014

Edge of Tomorrow *(feature film)*
Special visual consultant

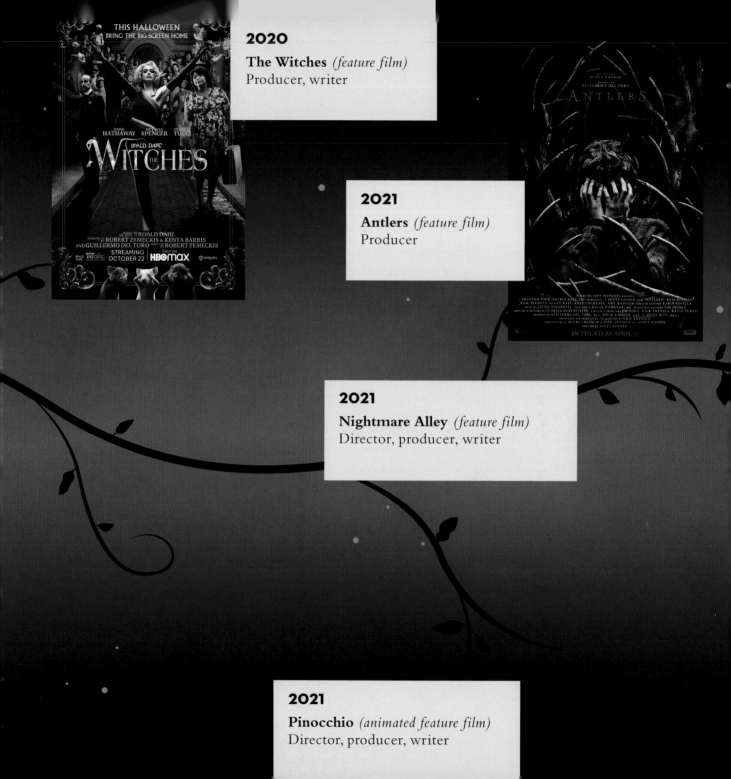

2020

The Witches *(feature film)*
Producer, writer

2021

Antlers *(feature film)*
Producer

2021

Nightmare Alley *(feature film)*
Director, producer, writer

2021

Pinocchio *(animated feature film)*
Director, producer, writer

Cut to sixty years later, and the Bureau for Paranormal Research and Defense's underground facility in New Jersey. Hellboy is all grown up (physically at least), and helping the secretive BPRD eliminate supernatural threats – usually by either punching them with his sledgehammer fist, known affectionately as The Right Hand of Doom, or blasting them with his supersized shooter, The Good Samaritan.

Hellboy's freak presence is being kept hidden from an outside world blissfully unaware of the paranormal. Not easy when he is the size of a bull and has a long red tail. His latest case, heralded by the arrival of a reptilian eyesore known as Sammael, sees yet another comeback for Rasputin, a coterie of undead Nazis, and a prophecy that Hellboy is due to bring about Armageddon.

The film cried out to be extravagant. Like a baroque Mexican church covered in gold leaf, enthused del Toro, 'the whole statement is excess.'[19]

There is a lot of Lovecraft in *Hellboy*. Mignola was a fellow disciple. It was another of the things that first drew del Toro to this musty branch of superhero lore. The design of the Sammael, with its tentacled snout and knack of splitting its essence when slain – QED: multiple Sammaels – was an offspring of del Toro's early sketches for *At the Mountains of Madness*. By the end of the film, as Rasputin re-opens portals to damnable planes, we see vast behemoths the size of planets, known as the Seven Gods of Chaos, that bear a more than passing resemblance to the Elder Gods from Lovecraft's Cthullu mythos.

It was equally important that the world of the film be self-contained. People could come in knowing nothing of the graphic novels and still feel at home in its cartoon excesses.

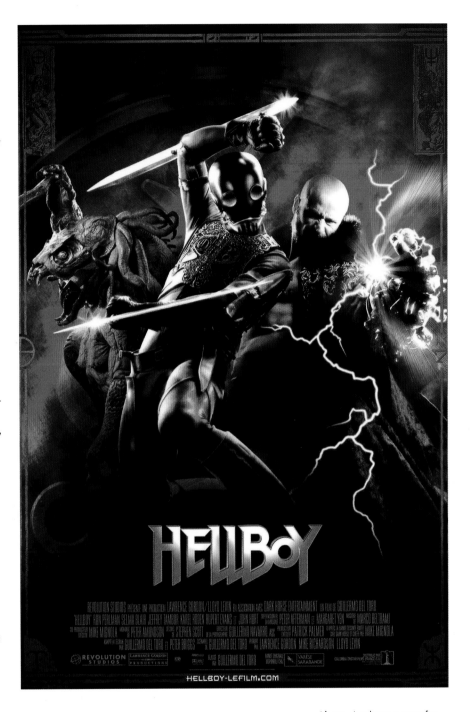

Above: A release poster for *Hellboy* highlighting the trio of unconventional villains: the demon Sammael, the balletic Kroenen, and the resurrected monk Rasputin (Karel Roden).

The screenplay has the cadence of a fairy tale with the 'once-upon-a-time' style of exposition conveyed via voice-over or dialogue info dumps. Rupert Evans's FBI greenhorn Myers is there essentially to be the incredulous eyes of the audience while he learns the ropes of BPRD protocol. 'There are things that go bump in the night,' explains Hurt's Professor. 'And we are the ones that bump back.'[20]

There is more than a dash of *Men in Black* to this droll matter-of-factness towards the supernatural. A further reason del Toro was so convinced about Perlman was that he knew no amount of scarlet body paint could stifle that deadpan personality. The whole film is tuned to the sardonic, pulp-cool attitude of the actor's performance. The subtext being that the diabolical Hellboy, and his eloquent merman sidekick Abraham 'Abe' Sapien (given graceful moves by Doug Jones and clipped voice by David Hyde Pierce) are very human.

Getting the correct red for Big Red was a challenge. 'I'll tell you,' lamented del Toro, 'one of the hardest things to do is to use a red character.'[21] Red needs to be very specific. 'Otherwise, you have a chocolate bar with an overcoat,'[22] he said. There are at least twenty shades of red in Hellboy, plus green and blue for the shading and liver spots (a trick borrowed from Lucian Freud's portraits).

For the overall look, del Toro took what was on the page and allowed room for Perlman. He added the Civil War duster coat, the long trousers (he couldn't see Perlman in shorts as per the comics), and the bedroom full of cats for company. As Hellboy snaffles Baby Ruth bars, guzzles beer, and pines for Liz, we are reminded he is still an adolescent.

There were elements of Mignola's original design that already felt

del Toro-esque: the Samurai topknot, the Victorian sideburns, the way the stumps of his filed-down horns resemble goggles perched on his brow. How del Toro loves goggles. They symbolize enhanced vision, a way of looking closer, and he himself has spent a lifetime behind glasses. Recall Dr. Mann's shattered glasses in *Mimic*,

Top: Despite his formidable prowess in fighting monsters, to del Toro, Hellboy was really just a lovesick teenager.

Above: Abe Sapien readies himself for some out-of-water investigation, which ironically necessitates the use of goggles.

a clockwork heart, hides his lidless eyes beneath the blackened portholes of his helmet.

Kroenen represents the apotheosis of the film's steampunk affectations. At one stage, del Toro had given him a ghostly form, allowing him to slink into the shadows. But the demands of the plot required a physical presence. What we see on screen was lifted from a mechanical assassin del Toro had designed for *The Left Hand of Darkness*: a wind-up man (or what's left of him) in a gold-plated armour, running on cogs and steam, his blood no more than dust. 'I wanted him to be like the embodiment of S&M,'[23] he said. Our one glimpse beneath the mask reveals little more than a patchwork skeleton with a lipless grin.

'I don't see myself ever doing a "normal" movie,' the director confessed. 'I love the creation of these *things* – I love the sculpting, I love the colouring. Half the joy is fabricating the world, the creatures.'[24]

It took an exhausting 130 days to create the world of *Hellboy*, still a record for del Toro. Each set comes infused with so much eye protein that the whole film vibrates with an inner energy and joy in the magic of its own creation. Before every scene, del Toro ritually walked into the space with the production designer to make final, incremental adjustments. Details only he could see.

Mignola was on set, at del Toro's request, in order to argue with him. 'Your duty is not to agree,' director informed writer. 'You convince me or I convince you.'[25] Del Toro would lose battles. When Hellboy first sneaks in through the cosmic gate, he had imagined a thirty-storey-high crib in which they find the Satanic baby, in tribute to *Rosemary's Baby*. Mignola winced, 'That's not consistent with the comic.'[26]

Above: Kroenen's exotic gold-plated armour, extendable blades, and diver's helmet were pure del Toro – he had sketches for just such a mechanical assassin figure going back to his earliest scripts.

or how Nyssa arrives disguised by the spiral irises of her ninja-style goggles in *Blade II*... or the Pale Man from *Pan's Labyrinth* slotting his eyes into his palms which are then held up to his face. In *Hellboy*, Abe has goggles to enable him to focus out of the water, and the Nazi assassin Karl Ruprecht Kroenen (Ladislav Beran), powered by

CGI intensified the visceral texture, with del Toro working to the Ray Harryhausen principle of locking the camera off and letting the monsters do their thing. Across the film, there were twelve or thirteen 'emblematic Hellboy moments and poses'[27] that he wanted to hit. For example: the sight of the hero bouncing skyward like a bionic kangaroo; the trajectory crashing him pinpoint into a subway shaft; a wrestling match with the Sammael in front of a statue in the museum; Hellboy plucking half a Russian corpse from his grave, and hauling him over his shoulder in order to provide directions. A fan favourite, this undead tour guide was known as The Corpse. Del Toro provided the voice himself.

The film comes to its world-splitting climax in Moscow, or to be more accurate beneath Moscow – in Rasputin's mausoleum augmented with giant cogs, spinning rooms, spiked traps, and gateways to the beyond. It's like stepping inside the Cronos Device. Del Toro reaches into himself and finds the Wagnerian grandeur,'[28] said *Slate*, applauding such gothic abandon. Here the universe will teeter on the brink of oblivion, waiting for Hellboy to make the right choice.

Del Toro doesn't consider himself to be a director in the populist vein of Steven Spielberg or James Cameron. I'm an acquired taste,'[29] he said. But that isn't entirely true. What he shares with those behemoths of the industry is their ability to touch something universal within their fantasies. *Hellboy* is a complex comic-book adventure lit up by lovely, idiosyncratic moments of human connection. Liz burning with

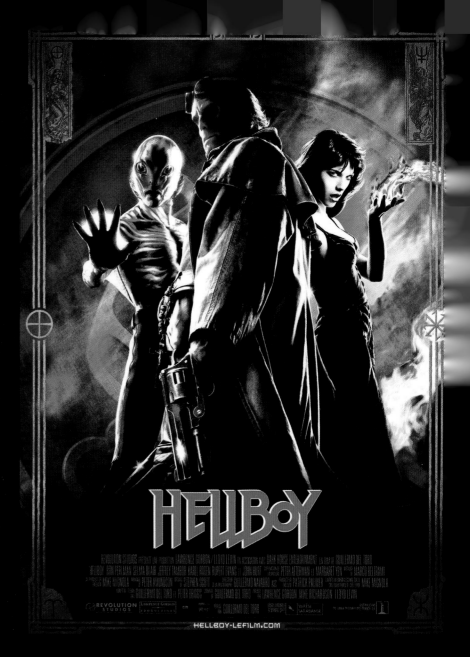

Above: A moody release poster introducing a trio of unconventional heroes – Abe Sapien, a shadowy Hellboy, and Liz, igniting blue flames

Opposite: With its fairy-tale themes, *Hellboy II: The Golden Army* would orientat back toward the director's natural predilections

In seeing beneath the skin of his fantastic creations, exploring the everyday quirks of a Twizzler-coloured demon, del Toro reminds us that we are all outsiders. That deep down we are all Hellboy.

With a final global tally of $99 million, it still proved a relatively niche proposition at the box office. But Hellboy refused to go quietly, and on DVD and Blu-ray (for the full benefit of the eye protein), a groundswell of appreciation grew. Moreover, in the wake of *The Lord of the Rings* and *Harry Potter*, fantasy had become big business. Thus, in 2008, Universal reclaimed their lost boy.

Returning to direct what is thus far his only sequel based on his own work, del Toro was in confident mood. *Pan's Labyrinth* was a sensation, and Hollywood was falling over itself to work with a director who combined the shine of arthouse respectability (with the added glint of international appeal) and mainstream success. Offers were being put to him. How about videogame adaptation *Halo?* Have you thought about *The Wolfman?* But he found himself stirred by the chance to look in on his favourite child, intrigued where a sequel might take the character. He also had $85 million to play with – a considerable amount, if still short of the $100 million-plus asking price of typical blockbusters.

With natural contrariness, del Toro's immediate thought was the love story. Or, to be more specific, the *relationship* story. 'So the second movie continues essentially after the big kiss,'[30] he explained, wondering how they were getting on. What has their first year of marriage been like? How is Liz dealing with living with a superheroic slob? Not well, it turns out. Plus, Hellboy is fraying against his enforced secrecy. He is facing up to being an adult.

Del Toro's latest monster-wrangling assignment was infected with all the research into myth and folklore he had done for *Pan's Labyrinth*. 'It's about the real world mining and undermining fantasy and magic,' he said, 'and how tragically we are destroying magic every day.'[31]

There had been a noticeable overlap in the active development of these two projects – such that del Toro considered them, spiritually, to be sister movies.

Shot over the winter of 2006 in Budapest, Hungary, *Hellboy II: The Golden Army* replaces Nazis with malcontent elves threatening to awaken an indestructible mechanical army, built eons ago by goblins, and resembling malevolent pocket watches. They would then lay waste to humanity. First, however, exiled elf Prince Nuada (Luke Goss) must unite the three pieces of the magical crown that commands these automated soldiers. Which is what brings him to New York.

Del Toro had struggled to find his story. Inspiration finally struck on a long car journey back from a family outing to Long Beach Aquarium, which he filled by expressing his worries to Mignola on the phone. 'The only thing that could work is if it is a rebellious prince,'[32] he told him, and they started 'jiving'[33] on the idea. By the end of the trip they were happily yelling ideas at each other. He needs a magical land! And a sidekick! The new structure offered an inversion of what had come before. The BPRD team would head into other worlds, giving it more of a fantasy feel, said del Toro, like *The Wizard of Oz*.

It was another epic undertaking at 120 days – including weeks of soul-sapping night shoots, and exponentially more creatures: meaning more stunt men overheating within heavy suits with limited sight-lines. Co-ordinating the enlarged bestiary drained the shoot of time and energy.

Above: With the look for elvish siblings Prince Nuada (Luke Goss) and Princess Nuala (Anna Walton), Guillermo del Toro was determined to deliver something far more formidable than the ethereal creatures of legend.

Opposite: For the sequel, the studio was far more confident to lead with the image of the scarlet hero in the marketing campaign, as well as his sardonic sense of humour.

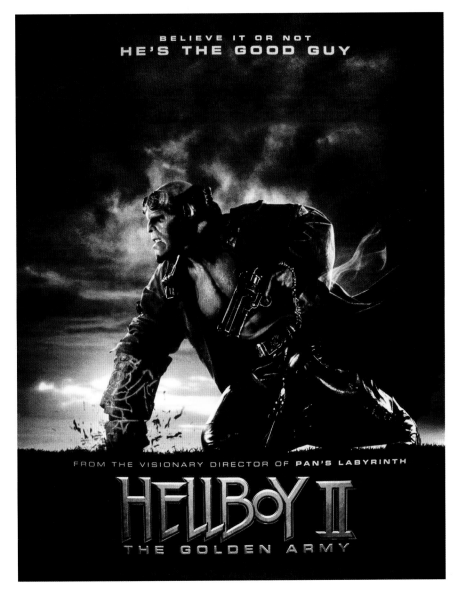

BELIEVE IT OR NOT
HE'S THE GOOD GUY

FROM THE VISIONARY DIRECTOR OF **PAN'S LABYRINTH**

HELLBOY II
THE GOLDEN ARMY

Nevertheless, del Toro felt liberated. He no longer needed to set up the rules of the world with acres of backstory. 'So you're allowed to have more fun,'[34] he said.

There were twenty to thirty notebook pages devoted to expanding the dual realities of *Hellboy*: human and monster. Thirty-two new creatures were designed and built: unless they were gigantic, such as The Last Elemental (a forest god that expands from a glowing seed to an orchid the size of three-storey building as if drawn by Hayao Miyazaki); or tiny, such as the swarming tooth fairies with rows of impeccable molars to gnaw though bone – both of which were made entirely out of CGI.

Del Toro wanted to escape from the prescribed notions of elves and trolls and fairies handed on by J.R.R. Tolkien and Arthur Rackham. The ivory faces and chiffon tresses of his elves are more sinister, even sicklier, than the supermodels of *The Lord of the Rings* movies. They appear more carvings than flesh. In a continuum of visual rhyming, this is the next stage of a strange porcelain motif begun with Jesús Gris in *Cronos*, continued with Santi in *The Devil's Backbone*, and into Nomak's Reapers in *Blade II*. Those designer vampires were clearly a trial run at his elves.

Of course, Nuada's errant prince also recalls Nomak's storyline. Using the same actor in Goss underlines the fact. Nuada is another complicated soul caught up in another family drama, and burdened with the film's themes. He is furious at the compromises made by his father King Balor (Roy Dotrice crowned with a set of antlers), sick of living in the shadow of eco-unfriendly humankind. His relationship with his sister, the kindlier Princess Nuala (Anna Walton), is both telepathic and borderline incestuous – not something you tended to see in Middle-earth.

'One idea I liked was to have the elf world in earth, gold, crimson and black, echoing the colours of Hellboy's library at the BPRD,' noted del Toro. 'That would emphasize the fact that Hellboy has something in common with the magic world.'[35]

Throughout the film, the director is staking out his turf. The mix of ironic foibles that keep Hellboy relatable is slotted within his brand of interconnected fabulation. Del Toro insisted on a more 'sensual'[36] quality. The Elemental, for instance, has the translucence of celery, and a fine coating of moss like the Faun in *Pan's Labyrinth*. And he wanted it painterly. The eye protein comes instilled with Pieter Brueghel, Arnold Böcklin and Hieronymus Bosch, as well as the Belgian Symbolists, the Surrealists, the Dadaists, and some of the Pop movement.

Top: One of the key images Guillermo del Toro wanted to retain from the comics was Hellboy's ability to use his tail to help him leap huge distances with precision.

Above: The Angel of Death (an uncredited Doug Jones) was created solely for the films and, in fact, was originally designed for an unmade del Toro film called *Mephisto's Bridge*.

Right: The Elemental, a giant sentient plant that grows to the height of a building, was one of the few instances where del Toro resorted to CGI to create his wonders.

Right: Better the devil you know – Guillermo del Toro and comic-book artist Mike Mignola share a joke at the premiere for *Hellboy II: The Golden Army.*

Opposite: Featured creatures – the heroic team along with Bethmoora Goblin (John Alexander) first cast eyes on the fabled Golden Army, hidden beneath the Giant's Causeway in Northern Ireland.

Mignola was the first to admit that the second film was 'much more a del Toro picture.'[37]

The shift in styles isn't always successful. The steampunk eccentricity and modern sass of the original tends to get drowned out by the florid developments. There is a lot of grotesque for the story to bear. Take the Troll Market, del Toro's riff on the Cantina scene in *Star Wars.* Located under Brooklyn Bridge if you know where to look, this was the Grimm Brothers at critical mass, a sprawling, creature-cluttered Expressionist bazaar impossible to take in. You start to crave the piercing clarity of *Pan's Labyrinth.*

It is here an increasingly cantankerous Hellboy (Perlman still relishing the assignment) takes on Nuada's sidekick, Mr. Wink (Brian Steele), a hulking cave troll with one eye sealed shut by a battle scar, and, in a mirror of his opponent, a giant metallic right fist. He was named after Selma Blair's one-eyed dog.

Del Toro wasn't entirely neglecting the comics. He returned to Mignola's pages to retrieve fan favourite Johann Krauss, a new addition officiously trying to bring order to the slipshod BPRD despite the fact he is a cloud of Germanic ectoplasm conveyed inside deep-sea diving gear. 'We went with a more Jules Verne containment suit type of look,'[38] said del Toro of the sequel's funniest addition.

Reviews were generally positive. It was beautifully done, but over-familiar. 'The film follows its predecessor's narrative arc with flow-chart precision,'[39] noted *The New Republic*: relics, battles, tragedies, and bureaucratic squabbles, before a big showdown in a giant clockwork crypt. The box office improved to $168 million. But hardly enough to turn heads. Marvel's *Iron Man*, released in the same year, finished with $585 million.

The third in a promised trilogy has never been realized. There were big ideas about *Hellboy* confronting the classic monsters from Universal's back catalogue of horror movies: the Wolf Man, Dracula and Frankenstein's monster, exactly as they appeared in the era of Bela Lugosi and Boris Karloff. Though that could have been del Toro dreaming out loud. His attention was taken by different projects. The shiniest of which was the chance to try and bend his inclinations toward a more established brand of fantasy.

RITES OF PASSAGE
Pan's Labyrinth (2006)

How he followed his heart back to Spain to conjure up a strange, arty mix of fairy tale and biting historical drama. Out of an intense and difficult shoot, like a butterfly from a cocoon, emerged the director's most adored film

Even with all his subsequent success, it may still be the happiest day of his professional life. As *Pan's Labyrinth* drew to its tragic yet hopeful close, the sound of applause rang in del Toro's ears like a benediction and didn't let up for a full twenty-four minutes – still the longest standing ovation in the history of the Cannes Film Festival. The reviews would follow suit, lavishing praise upon this career-defining synthesis of history and myth.

'I don't see why it shouldn't sit on the same altar of High Fantasy as the *Lord of the Rings* trilogy – it's that worthy,'[1] exclaimed *Entertainment Weekly*.

The New York Times intuited the profound questions being posed by its monstrous visions. '*Pan's Labyrinth* is a political fable in the guise of a fairy tale. Or maybe it's the other way around. Does the moral structure of the children's story illuminate the nature of authoritarian rule? Or does the movie reveal fascism as a terrible fairy tale brought to life?'[2]

In one of those aberrations of film history, del Toro would lose the festival's highest honour, the Palme d'Or, to Ken Loach's dreary Irish drama *The Wind That Shakes the Barley*, while directing honours went to fellow Mexican and amigo Alejandro González Iñárritu for *Babel*. But there was no doubt that the world had finally woken up to the fact that beneath the fan-boy exuberance was an artist.

Above: As with all Guillermo del Toro films, magic reveals itself quickly. On her very first night at the mill, Ofelia (Ivana Baquero) shows her book of fairy tales to an actual fairy.

Opposite: Perhaps the defining image of not only *Pan's Labyrinth*, but del Toro's entire career. Ofelia encounters the beguiling Faun (Doug Jones), who sets her three tasks, mixing the worlds of reality and fantasy.

For Guillermo del Toro, a labyrinth was not a place where you became lost, but somewhere you found your way. 'After many twists and turns and moments of despair,'[3] he added; that is, after all, the weft of storytelling. From Greek myth to Lewis Carroll's Wonderland, cathedral floors to country gardens, the subway warrens of *Mimic* to the sewers of *Blade II*, he had been consumed with the metaphorical power of the labyrinthine. You might say it was a state of mind.

The journey to his signature triumph was fraught with test and tribulation, and despair. After *Mimic*, he said, '*Pan's Labyrinth* was the second most painful film to make.'[4] Difficult conditions, producer interference, malfunctioning toads, and a minimal budget were pitted against unquenchable ambition. It was a film that should not have been attempted, he (later) grinned, 'If you listen to reason, that is…'[5]

During a brief spell in London in 2002, del Toro met another old amigo, Alfonso Cuarón, for dinner. At the time, he was in pre-production on *Hellboy*; Cuarón was shooting *Harry Potter and the Prisoner of Azkaban*. There had been overtures from Warner Bros. about handing del Toro the reins to the lucrative franchise. You can see the thinking: he drank deep from the same primordial-mythological soup from which J.K. Rowling had been spooning inspiration. Learning that Cuarón had been offered the third in the series without having read a single entry in Rowling's canon, an irate del Toro had manhandled his friend to the nearest bookstore to rectify the situation. He took magic seriously. Maybe *too* seriously.

Del Toro's take on *Harry Potter* wasn't quite on the same wavelength as the studio's. 'I saw [the books] as deeper, more creaky, more corroded,'[6] he said, likening them to Dickens. He also proposed killing one of the kids, most likely Ron Weasley, to add a bit of dramatic heft.

In any case, he had a much earthier, more allusive and personal form of magic in mind, and on that warm London night, fuelled by good wine,

Opposite below: A Mexican revolutionary – in his signature film Guillermo del Toro perfected a new cinematic language by juxtaposing cold historical fact with the magic of fairy tales.

Right: Fellow countryman Alfonso Cuarón on the set of *Harry Potter and the Prisoner of Azkaban*. It was Cuarón who initially encouraged del Toro to pursue *Pan's Labyrinth,* serving as producer on the iconic project.

he regaled Cuarón with the story of *Pan's Labyrinth*. The entire film was already there, marvelled Cuarón, a culmination of all del Toro's thematic preoccupations: family, religion, myth, isolated children, and those same scars, left by the Spanish Civil War, that had run through *The Devil's Backbone*. Ultimately, del Toro informed his friend, it was 'about the permeability of the membrane between reality and fantasy.'[7]

Opening in 1944, five years after General Franco's fascist victory has riven Spain, we meet eleven-year-old Ofelia (Ivana Baquero) on the back seat of a car, her attention consumed by a book of fairy tales. Del Toro is once again looking at the world through the large, dark eyes of a child. Those 'ambassadors of a higher culture,'[8] as he liked to say. Ofelia is on her way to live in an old mill with her pregnant mother, Carmen (Ariadna Gil), and wicked stepfather, Captain Vidal (Sergi López), an officer in Franco's army. Cruel as a knife-edge, he has been stationed at this forested outpost in Galicia to hunt

Republican insurgents – the *maquis* – hidden among the trees. In this untamed landscape, at the heart of a stone labyrinth, Ofelia will discover a portal to a fabulous underworld realm and an extraordinary gatekeeper in the shape of the Faun (Doug Jones). Slender as a sapling, his voice sly with enchantment, the Faun sets her three daunting tasks in order to open the doorway.

As with all del Toro's *sui generis* work, the story was born through an imaginative chain reaction. Around 2003, he had been reading a lot of fairy tales, as well as more analytical books such as Edwin Sidney Hartland's *The Science of Fairy Tales*, a catalogue of what del Toro called 'the primordial streaks of storytelling in fairy-tale lore.'[9] In particular, he had fallen deep into the stories of early twentieth century British fabulists Algernon Blackwood and Arthur Machen (both also members of the Hermetic Order of the Golden Dawn, devoted to studying the paranormal) and was 'very attracted'[10] by the idea that savage pagan mythologies lie beneath

the surface of the modern world. In northern Spain, he learned, there remains a huge Celtic footprint. 'And it's interesting, as I don't see much of this in Spanish cinema... So I thought it would be great to do a period piece set there.'[11]

Cuarón knew that the origins to *Pan's Labyrinth* also lay back in *La Hora Marcada*, the horror anthology series on which they cut their teeth. An episode called *De Ogros (About Ogres)*, written by del Toro and directed by Cuarón, followed a small girl who chooses to live with an ogre in the city sewers instead of remaining with her abusive father. 'She preferred the monster rather than the monstrosity of her father,'[12] said del Toro. This slim tale has served as an outline for many subsequent feature films.

The true genesis of Ofelia's adventures lay in the landscape of del Toro's childhood. 'I have spent thirty-two years recuperating from my first ten years,' he told an audience at the British Film Institute in London, who were unsure whether to laugh. 'Really,' he insisted. 'I had a pretty

screwed-up childhood... I don't know if it's because I was living in Mexico and I'm a Mexican but I have had a life full of very, very fucked-up and strange things.'[13]

When he was twelve, he heard a beloved uncle whispering to him from beyond the grave. Not words, exactly, more of a sigh. They had been good friends. His uncle had introduced him to H.P. Lovecraft. The rational part of del Toro's brain argued it must be a draught, but the windows were shut. And even in bed, he could hear the same sigh coming from inside

the mattress. That experience stirred Santi's midnight whisperings in *The Devil's Backbone*.

Younger still, he would often sleep at his grandmother's old Mexican house with its long, shadowy corridors. Longer to a child's mind – like the passageway that stretches between Ofelia and freedom when the Pale Man awakens, slots his eyeballs back into the palms of his hands, and comes lumbering in pursuit. 'And every night, punctually at midnight, in my bedroom, a faun would come out of the armoire,' he recounted, as if this

was entirely to be expected from a sleepover at grandma's house. 'It must have been lucid dreaming, but for a child, it was as if it was real. I saw him.'[14] He wasn't quite the jaunty, teasing, chatterbox Faun who greets us in *Pan's Labyrinth*. The human hands and a grinning goat's face suggested a far more malevolent persona.

'There are all those figures in the iconography of Mexico of the Devil being a sort of upright goat,'[15] recognized del Toro, who, despite the movie's title, clarified that his character was *not* a version of the god

Opposite: Ofelia begins the second test in the halls of the Pale Man. The long corridor was another nightmare vision channelled directly from Guillermo del Toro's childhood.

Below: Creating the perfect mix of human and animal in the Faun (Doug Jones) was one of the biggest challenges of the director's career.

Pan of pagan legend. The title had been invented to appease foreign distributors.

Then there was the starkly adult effect of 9/11. Only days before the planes struck the towers, del Toro had presented *The Devil's Backbone* at the Toronto Film Festival, leaving buoyed by rave reviews. 'Cloaked in my petit bourgeois happiness at how well my film was received,'[16] he said. At home, watching the terrible events unfold on television with his wife and family close, all he could do was weep. The world, he knew, had shifted beyond recognition. Or maybe revealed its true nature. His only answer was to make a companion film to *The Devil's Backbone*, to use his art once again to process history's cycles of brutality. Only this would be a sister film, filled with female energy.

'I wanted to make it because fascism is definitely a male concern and a boy's game,' he said, 'so I wanted to oppose that with an eleven-year-old girl's universe.'[17]

An early version of *Pan's Labyrinth* had centred on a wife who has fallen pregnant. She then falls in love with the Faun, who requires her to sacrifice the child, promising that she will find her son on the other side. 'And she made that leap of faith,' said del Toro. 'It was a shocking tale.'[18] The skeleton of that concept still exists in Ofelia's heavily pregnant mother in thrall to her loveless husband, but it had evolved to become Ofelia's story. Something he hadn't fully realized until he sat down with Cuarón.

While in keeping with the tone and child's-eye view of *Cronos*, *Pan's Labyrinth* was specifically a mirror to *The Devil's Backbone*. Both reside in the protracted tragedy and political labyrinth of the Spanish Civil War. Both draw narrative sustenance from the landscape, though now it is a wintery, arboreal setting compared to the orphanage's desert backdrop. Both commence with a lonely child being driven to a forbidding new location. Both study the horrors of war from beneath the veil of the supernatural. And both were shot and financed in Spain. That was something else he iterated to Cuarón. How determined he was to shoot in his native Spanish.

A temptingly rich offer had been put to him by Universal, on condition that he made the film in English. But this was about maintaining an underdog sensibility with a touch of European magic. The intimacy of the story mattered. 'I thought, I want to tell a story of which there is no trace,' he said. 'I don't want to talk about a big story of the war, but a very small story about the heroes and villains.'[19] All these characters, he knew, would disappear into the flow of history.

On some level, del Toro needed to struggle. To evoke what lay *underneath* the story – the belief that compassion and identity must prevail over the conformity and cruelty of fascism. 'Blind obedience castrates, negates, hides, and destroys what makes us human,'[20] he insisted. On a purely artistic level, there is nothing more shocking to his system than the stifling of creative freedom.

Set five years earlier, *The Devil's Backbone* had examined the overall tragedy of the Spanish Civil War in miniature like a slide beneath a microscope. Whereas *Pan's Labyrinth*, insisted del Toro, was about 'choice and disobedience.'[21] Ofelia, channelling her creator's spirit of rebellion, will find hidden depths to resist monsters in both the real and fantastical worlds, joining the ranks of a grand tradition.

'We are doing homages to Lewis Carroll, to *The Wizard of Oz*, to Hans Christian Andersen with *The Little Matchstick Girl*, to Oscar Wilde, and very specifically to *David Copperfield* and Charles Dickens,'[22] said del Toro. In a film of multiple interpretations like turns in a maze, there are numerous cinematic and literary references to guide you through. How could it be otherwise? This is del Toro.

They ranged across the spectrum from Neil Jordan's Freudian beasts in *The Company of Wolves* to Jim Henson's Muppety escapade *Labyrinth*, in which Jennifer Connelly must traverse a riddling maze to rescue

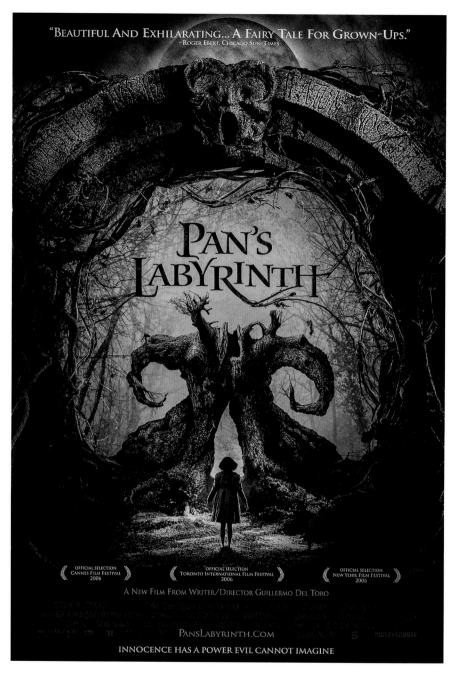

Above: The film's poster has become celebrated in its own right – the rhyming of the tree branches with fallopian tubes led some wags to rechristen the film *A Womb With A View*.

Opposite above: Captain Vidal (Sergi López) inspects the handiwork of the Republican guerrillas. The director wanted his villain to be pristine, down to the creak of his leather gloves.

her baby brother from the hands of David Bowie's goblin king. The pretty party dress Ofelia ruins while exploring the woods is a replica of the one worn by the heroine in Disney's animated 1951 version of *Alice in Wonderland*, only in green. The very name Ofelia recalls both Hamlet's doomed love and the daughter of Roald Dahl – the writer's blackly comic flights of fantasy are yet another prevailing influence on the director.

In Spanish terms, Buñuel's presence can be felt in the depictions of the wealthy guests and local priest sitting down to dine with fascists as the peasants starve. But del Toro's most pertinent influence of all is *The Spirit of the Beehive*, Victor Erice's

lyrical study of childhood made under Franco's shadow in 1973. 'A movie that transformed my life,'[23] he sighed as if speaking about a lover. Set in 1940, *The Spirit of the Beehive* is about a six-year-old girl (Ana Torrent) whose life is transformed when she sees *Frankenstein*. Del Toro became tiny Ana (as he is Ofelia), searching for the monster in a wounded Spanish landscape, only to find a Republican deserter hiding in a remote sheep-shed, secretly provisioning him with food and clothing and her father's watch.

'The way I cast children is defined by this movie,'[24] said del Toro. The eyes of the elfin Torrent, he explained, were capable of 'seeing mysteries.'[25] Here was 'the most sacred spirit of

films.'[26] A purity he hoped to instil within *Pan's Labyrinth*.

As their dinner in London drew to an end, Cuarón's reaction was immediate. Del Toro was dispatched to set down his wonderful tale in script form, while he began the search for independent financing as producer.

A few months later, things almost came to an abrupt halt when del Toro left his most recent notebook in the back of a London cab. This proved a pivotal moment in his career. A crossroads. For one thing, he was tight for money. The potential budget for *Pan's Labyrinth* had yet to materialize, and an email had landed in his inbox offering him all the riches of the Hollywood machine. It was from

Marvel, and before del Toro, much like the banquet on the Pale Man's treacherous table, was laid a choice of *X-Men 3*, *Fantastic Four*, or *Thor*. 'Big, big movies,'[27] he acknowledged, and very well paid. It was so tempting. Maybe he could lose himself to one of these blockbusters and then return to *Pan's Labyrinth*?

But the sudden loss of the notebook was like having part of his brain torn out. Sat in his hotel room, he wept. All his notebooks are crucial to his creative process – in the early stages of a film, they *are* his creative process – but this latest copy represented a blueprint for the entire world and philosophy of *Pan's Labyrinth*. Then the phone rang. The cab driver in

question was a resourceful soul. Finding they had shared interests, del Toro had left him with the address to a comic-book store scribbled on hotel stationery. He had spotted the logo and tracked him down, notebook in hand. Del Toro was convinced this was destiny. 'I was about to lose myself,'[28] he thought. He had to make *Pan's Labyrinth*.

Filling the inky pages of his reclaimed notebook was a familiar exploration of story ideas: entire scenes, specific shots and designs, lines of dialogue, all his wonderful tumbling thoughts. Concepts for a second *Hellboy* nudged their way onto the same page, the two films bleeding together. But it was clear that Ofelia's

tale was now an obsession. Here were details that would be lost along the way, or transformed by creative mutation. At one stage, elves were to make off with the baby, leaving a changeling in his place (formed from mandrake root). There were plans for ghost children – no more than heads, perched on a latticework of feathery nerves, which would consume the fairies. In the finished film, it is the Pale Man who will tear into fairy flesh in a horrific re-enactment of Goya's *Saturn Devouring His Son*; the nineteenth-century painting that came to embody the idea of Spain consuming itself in the Civil War.

It was all too much. This couldn't be a film that gorged on his imagination

Opposite: The terrifying Pale Man (Doug Jones) had many inspirations, one of them being Guillermo del Toro himself. He had lost a lot of weight before the production, saw how his skin was sagging, and applied the idea as a metaphor for starving Spain.

Right: Goya's famous painting of *Saturn Devouring His Son* was another key influence in the depiction of the Pale Man.

Below: Ofelia (Ivana Baquero), clutching her baby brother, faces her final test at the centre of the labyrinth, uniting the realms of the Captain (Sergi López) and the Faun (Doug Jones).

like *Hellboy*. *Pan's Labyrinth* required the restraint of *The Devil's Backbone*. It was a story located in a brutal historical reality. The fantastical elements would be all the more effective – and real – for their concentration on the Faun, his fairy emissaries, and the three tasks Ofelia must complete in order to resume her rightful place as princess of the Underworld.

Finding the perfect Ofelia represented a huge risk. Del Toro was essentially placing his entire film in the hands of a girl he had never met. Taking a more psychological sounding on the story, Ofelia must make her way to her own centre – her true self – to escape the binds of reality. 'Which I think is very real,'[29] said del Toro.

At 11, Ivana Baquero was older than the eight-year-old street urchin he had in mind, but her dark eyes stood out from a thousand potential young actresses. Going back to Tamara Shanath in *Cronos*, del Toro auditions his child actors the same way. When they walk in, he has them look around the room, then straight at him. There would be some customary talk, but he would already know. Baquero had the same magical way of looking as Ana in *The Spirit of the Beehive*. As the meeting ended, he picked up a copy of the script and handed it to her. 'If you want the role,' he smiled, 'it's yours.'[30]

For one so young, Baquero had a worldly air. A pupil at the American School of Barcelona, she was already a proven actress with three films to her name, including the English-language ghost story *Fragile*. It was important, that hint of an old soul. There was a fierceness to her too, a quick flash of fire in those eyes. Then she could smile and steal every heart in the room. Del Toro provided a steady stream of books and comics to assimilate her into his world.

Left: Victor Erice's sublime Spanish Civil War drama *The Spirit of the Beehive*, starring Ana Torrent as the young Ana and Teresa Gimpera as her mother, is a profound influence on both Guillermo del Toro and *Pan's Labyrinth*.

Opposite: Ofelia (Ivana Baquero) faces the slumbering Pale Man presiding over a lavish feast. Within the intricate schemes of del Toro's symbolism, all the food is blood red in colour.

One of many theories rising like mist from the film's cult following is that housekeeper and clandestine revolutionary Mercedes (a strident Maribel Verdú, from Cuarón's *Y Tu Mamá También*) is a vision of the future Ofelia. 'My mother told me to be wary of fauns,'[31] she tells Ofelia.

On her first night at the mill, Ofelia receives a visitation. Not a ghost in this case, but a fairy, transforming from the guise of a stick insect like the metamorphic roaches in *Mimic*. The digitally conjured fairies of *Pan's Labyrinth* are identical in appearance to the three sprites seen pickled in a jar in *Hellboy*: eight inches tall, variable body colour, hairless, pointy-eared, and with leaf-like wings. The vicious tooth fairies that swarm into *Hellboy II* confirm the prevalent form for this crossover species. They are an extension of del Toro's trope of chittering insects.

The fairy will guide Ofelia to the sunken chamber in the labyrinth to be greeted by the Faun, the film's unforgettable trickster, towering on zigzag legs, who will set the rules of the game. While the story would feel as ancient as the ruins, like something passed from generation to generation, del Toro needed his creature design to be fresh and beautiful. Having made his way through meatier, more humanoid and ancient-goat design stages, the Faun is a conflation of devil, jester, a sketch by Machen, and one of Tolkien's Ents, with a sprinkling of H.R. Giger's *Alien* DNA in his mossy limbs.

Sealed inside the specially engineered suit (designed by the director), Doug Jones could express the full range of his sinuous, alien body language (the character's archaic Castilian speech was voiced, in the end, by stage actor Pablo Adán). Del Toro wanted the slippery Faun to have the lithesome, shifty allure of a rock star. 'More Mick Jagger, less David Bowie,'[32] he charged his collaborator. Likewise, if he ever gets the greenlight for his long-sought adaptation of the Mary Shelley classic, he has promised the 'Iggy Pop of Frankensteins!'[33]

A month after shooting began, the Faun made his debut on set. There was complete silence, then applause. Even weeks later, the crew struggled to take their eyes off him. It was as if he had them hypnotized.

To evoke how porous the border is between otherness and reality, the image of the faun was subtly invoked in bannisters, doorframes and handles, as well as symbols of occult lore like owls. But 'it's very, very subtle,'[34] warned del Toro.

The horns are elaborately curved like fallopian tubes, a womanly motif that will be repeated in the shape of the shattered tree where Ofelia must complete her first task, and once again on the film's distinctive poster. It reinforces del Toro's female orientation – the power to create life. The director laughed. 'When we did the poster for Cannes, somebody said they wanted to call the movie *A Womb With A View*. The idea is that this girl's idea of heaven, ultimately, is to go back into her mother's belly.'[35]

The First Task: by the Faun's instructions, Ofelia must reclaim a key from the belly of an odious toad that lives beneath the aforementioned tree, into which she must scramble

like Alice into Wonderland. Though this dank tunnel of tangled roots is far less salubrious. The animatronic toad was the size of a baby hippo, and too cumbersome for Ofelia to leap onto his head as planned, so del Toro hastily readjusted the scene to have the reluctant amphibian spew up some CGI entrails, having been fed indigestible magic stones.

'The fantasy world of *Pan's Labyrinth* is oppressive!' he insisted, justifying this splash of *Hellboy* grunge across his poetic canvas. 'The frog, the Pale Man, the fairies who are grimy and eat raw meat – it's not exactly Jim Henson, you know.'[36]

The Second Task: using a stick of magic chalk to manifest a door in the wall (another gateway between worlds), Ofelia must venture into the fresco-lined chambers of the Pale Man, a grotesque apparition slumbering before a vast banquet. His eyeballs sit in front of him on a plate.

While resisting the temptations of the delicious food, Ofelia must use the golden key to retrieve a dagger, the magical half of the story moving to the tidy rhythms of cause and effect pioneered by the Brothers Grimm.

Amid the startling bestiary that del Toro has made his life's calling, the Pale Man remains his most primal and terrifying of creations. He had evolved from an elderly figure with wooden hands into the faceless chalk-white fiend with sagging flesh (modelled on the folds in del Toro's thinning body) and hands that have stigmata-like slits into which to insert his eyeballs – a horrific image that sprang from his memories of the statues of Saint Lucia, who had her eyeballs gouged out, and tends to be portrayed carrying them on a dish, with her sockets bleeding. The Catholic Church is the gift that keeps on giving. Beneath the mask was Jones once more.

Citing the creature's multipurpose symbolism, del Toro made clear that the Pale Man 'represents fascism and the Church eating the children when they have a perversely abundant banquet in front of them. There is almost a hunger to eat innocence. A hunger to eat purity.'[37]

A powerful visual rhyme is formed between the Pale Man's feast and Vidal's dinner party at the mill, with church and state as his guests. Note how both Pale Man and Vidal are sat in the same position at the head of the table framed against a blazing fire. The point is clear: the menagerie of creatures, particularly the Pale Man, reflects the film's true monster – in human form. Captain Vidal, played with icy menace by Sergi López (better known as a comic actor) is the chilling representative of Franco, indeed all male authoritarians, coated in the slick veneer of fascism.

Del Toro saw him as the man Jacinto, the lost prince in *The Devil's Backbone*, might have become. Both are portrayed as virile and handsome. 'One of the dangers of fascism and one of the dangers of true evil in our world – which I believe exists – is that it's very attractive,'[38] said del Toro. His instruction to López was to always look elegant. There is a lovely bit of sound editing in the ominous creak of his leather boots and gloves.

'I don't write the bad guys in my movies without knowing what they feel,'[39] insisted del Toro. Vidal has rejected magic and fiction, craving only order and purity. He is blindly psychopathic, a coiled spring – and the film does not flinch from his violence – but like Jacinto he has a complex pathology. That compulsive cleaning of his father's fob watch (a trinket as polished and intricate as the Cronos Device) reveals a man trapped in the legacy of a great Franco general who had died honourably in battle. Or as del Toro put it, Vidal has been dropped into his own 'historical labyrinth'[40] from which he cannot escape.

By refusing the studio dollar, del Toro spoke of 'trying to redefine my life, creatively.'[41] But freedom proved an uphill struggle. Shooting through the summer of 2005, the slender budget of $14 million fell far short of his ambitions. 'A budget is a state of mind,'[42] he told himself. Whether you have $19 million or $190 million, your vision must hunger for more. As he had on *Cronos*, he found a way almost by

sheer willpower, ploughing his fee back into the film. That he was also co-producer brought with it a state of constant anxiety, sleeping three hours a night, and losing weight. 'And most of the crew thought we were making a strange silly movie,'[43] he said.

Add to this drought conditions in the formidable Scots Pine forests of Guadarrama Mountains, not far from Madrid. With the risk of fire, there were restrictions put on explosions and gunfire. 'And we were a war movie!'[44] groaned del Toro. A complex irrigation system had to be installed to make the grass grow. The cadre of Spanish financiers, convinced he was out of control, schemed to shut the production down. On one level, it was true. Del Toro was perpetually unsatisfied with what he saw in the frame. He wondered if his demands were growing tyrannical.

'It is the duty of the filmmaker to remain unreasonable,'[45] he said. To save money, he employed untested department heads and fledgling effects companies, hoping they would be as hungry as he had been at the start. But there were bruising creative encounters. Everything had to be made from scratch: sets, props, furniture, and the entire wardrobe. All to del Toro's exacting specifications, where reality was every bit as meaningful as fantasy. The mill and its outbuildings that make up Vidal's crumbling fortress were built in situ.

'I follow a principle that I got from theatrical design: each set has to make one statement,'[46] he said. They need to be read quickly and make their storytelling point. The point made by the central patio in *The Devil's Backbone* is the unexploded bomb. In the Pale Man's chambers the point is the chimney and the fireplace. In Vidal's office our eyes are drawn to the great gears that fill the back wall like a giant eyeball. Those wheels resonate with all the infernal machines that drive the worlds of del Toro's making. 'They represent, I think, the mechanism of the universe,' he said, 'cyclical nature, the inexorable.'[47] They are also echoes of the delicate cogs inside Vidal's watch. Further proof that the captain is trapped inside that timepiece.

The Final Task: most awful of all, Ofelia must shed a drop of blood from her newborn brother, to whom she has been telling stories while he is safely stowed in his mother's womb in a brush of pink CGI. This will bring her into a terrible and final confrontation with both the Faun and a crazed Vidal beneath the glare of a full moon.

Above: Guillermo del Toro provides direction for Sergi López as Captain Vidal. The Captain's office backs onto the mill's giant clockwork machinery designed to resemble a huge eye.

Opposite: As soon as Ivana Baquero walked into her audition, del Toro knew she was the perfect Ofelia. Amongst her many qualities, straightway she reminded him of Ana Torrent in *The Spirit of the Beehive*.

James Cameron was among the first to see a cut of the film. Whenever either of them was close to delivering their film, a ritual had been established where the other would be there to offer advice. A culture of support among Mexican filmmakers del Toro had brought to Hollywood. 'He always said that when somebody was finishing a film, it was like a baby being born,' said Cameron. 'You're going through labour and everyone gathers to support.'[48] How different it was from American filmmakers, prowling the ward like wolves. Like Cuarón, Cameron could see a new maturity. 'It felt like something he had been building toward,'[49] he said.

After Cannes, *Pan's Labyrinth* would grow into an international sensation, making $84 million worldwide, and becoming the most successful Spanish language film ever released in America. Del Toro's reputation was sealed. Though he was unlucky again to miss out on the Oscar for Best Foreign Language Film, this time to the excellent German thriller *The Lives of Others*, exploring similar themes of art and identity in the shadow of an oppressive regime.

One of the many things that makes the film so special is what Mar Diestro-Dópido, in her *BFI Film Classic*, called its 'unapologetic ambiguity.'[50] Exactly the kind of evocative magic that stirs a cult following. Equally, academic interpretations have bloomed from such fertile soil. Could it have been a study of the crisis in capitalism in a post-9/11 world? An exploration of the fantasy Franco imposed upon Spain?

'I marvelled at the fact that fairy tales and fantasy are considered "childish" endeavours,' said del Toro, 'while war is viewed as a noble and adult quest.'[51]

Perhaps the most pertinent question is how much of *Pan's Labyrinth* exists only in Ofelia's head. As with the uncertainties of *Alice in Wonderland* and *The Wizard of Oz*, there are hints either way. The real and mystical come carefully entwined. Everything tallies: human monsters with grotesque beasts; pagan mythologies with Catholic doctrine; how the fantasy is bathed in warm, humid, earthy colours, while reality is cold as steel, thanks to cinematographer Guillermo Navarro. Yet Vidal cannot see the Faun.

'Fantasy is a language that allows us to explain, interpret and reappropriate reality,' proposed del Toro. *Pan's Labyrinth*, he insisted, is like a Rorschach test. 'If the movie works as a piece of storytelling, as a piece of artistic creation, it should tell something different to everyone. It should be a matter of personal discussion. Now objectively, the way I structured it, there are three clues in the movie that tell you where I stand.'[52]

Del Toro's Clues: firstly, the fact that there is no other way than the chalk door to get from the attic to Vidal's office. Secondly, the walls opening up as Ofelia flees Vidal through the labyrinth (as Danny flees his father through the maze in *The Shining*) create enough real distance to prevent him from catching her. Finally, there is the white flower blooming in remembrance at the very end.

'I stand by the fantasy,'[53] he declared, as if delivering a creed.

Above: Doug Jones as the iconic Faun, who in the grand tradition of Guillermo del Toro's wondrous creations is less a monster than a double-edged character – both enchanting and deceptive.

Right: Ofelia retrieves the magical dagger – a shot that conveys the powerful contrasts of the director's use of colour, with the earth-tones of the walls, the aquamarine of the girl's dress, the gold dagger, and the crimson of the cloth.

HIGH CONCEPT

Pacific Rim (2013)

How after five years consumed by failed projects and heartbreak, he rekindled his mojo with the biggest movie he could imagine: giant robots fighting giant monsters against a thrilling dystopian backdrop

There was a time when Guillermo del Toro feared he might become better known for the films he didn't make. Even the most successful directors – even a Spielberg or Cameron – leave a trail of thwarted dreams in their wake.

The precarious nature of the business, slave to the whims of studio executives and the prognostications of their number-crunching soothsayers, requires filmmakers to keep their options open. If only to stay sane, you needed to spread the love.

What makes del Toro unusual among his peers is the openness and passion with which he discusses his potential projects. So much so that an entire mythology has grown up around what might be called the unborn films of Guillermo del Toro.

By 2017, he calculated that he had written twenty-four screenplays and made only ten movies. Preserved like foetuses in a jar, each of the remaining fourteen hypothetical wonders not only encompassed a screenplay, but screeds of designs, animatics, sculptures, location scouting, casting even, as well as emotional investment. Whispering from the wings, they confirm the underlying synergy between everything he does. As we have seen, del Toro will happily strip an unmade script for parts.

Right: Raleigh Becket (Charlie Hunnam) and Mako Mori (Rinko Kikuchi) pilot a giant Jaeger robot by linking their minds in a process called 'drift'.

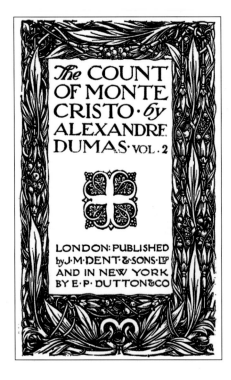

'I remember reading Raymond Chandler in his entirety and realizing that he cannibalized his stories,' he casually pointed out. 'He would take a paragraph from his first detective, who was called John Dalmas, and he would reuse that paragraph, and make it better, like fifteen years later.'[1]

The beautiful dance in *Crimson Peak* in which Tom Hiddleston manages, just, to keep his candle alight was first proposed for *The Left Hand of Darkness* in 1993. Familiar from previous chapters, the director's take on *The Count of Monte Cristo* is one of a quartet of lost films that speak loudest to what we understand as del Toro-esque. Three represent the most crushing disappointments of his career, though we cling to the hope they may yet see the comforting dark of a movie house. The other is a tale of what could have been but never will.

Written between 1993 and 1998, but most intensely during the bleak days of his father's kidnap, del Toro

admitted *The Left Hand of Darkness* contains 'a lot of rage.'[2] The bond between fathers and sons is central. The scope, meanwhile, is ambitious (read: expensive). 'I'm very, very proud of the screenplay,' he has said – as he should be: it's a great well of storytelling and literary allusion. 'But it requires a set of tools that are a little daunting. It's sort of like a David Lean-Sergio Leone epic western. Very much full of magic. And it's the only movie without any creatures.'[3]

The story begins on the Mexican border in 1862 – 'a time and a place ripe for treason,'[4] relishes the script. The mood is gothic, ornate, with clockwork contraptions and flickers of mysticism. 'I've always thought that Dumas wanted to evoke the spirit of *1001 Nights*, his fascination for the Orient,'[5] said del Toro. Previous versions had lacked that exoticism. In the book, the Count is variously described as a 'pirate,' a 'vampire,' and a 'thief.'[6] His version of the hero,

Edmundo Dantes, only travels by night in Blade-like sunglasses and cape. 'He's very close to a Dracula coming from a Western,' mused the director, 'all dressed in black, red and gold. He has a mechanical arm that allows him to draw faster than every one.'[7]

Notions of death and resurrection reoccur. Del Toro called it very Catholic. By the end, amid a symbolic sandstorm, the hero is close to demented, his enemy's bullets having no effect.

Asked why his Mexican epic had never come to pass, del Toro could only shrug. 'It never seems to be the right time,'[8] he said. Maybe it was that bit too ambitious. Maybe 1998's *The Mask of Zorro*, so similar in style, stole its thunder. Just maybe the right time is still to come.

As far back as he can remember, del Toro has dreamed of adapting Mary Shelley's *Frankenstein*. This was the foundational text of modern monster mythology. Before the

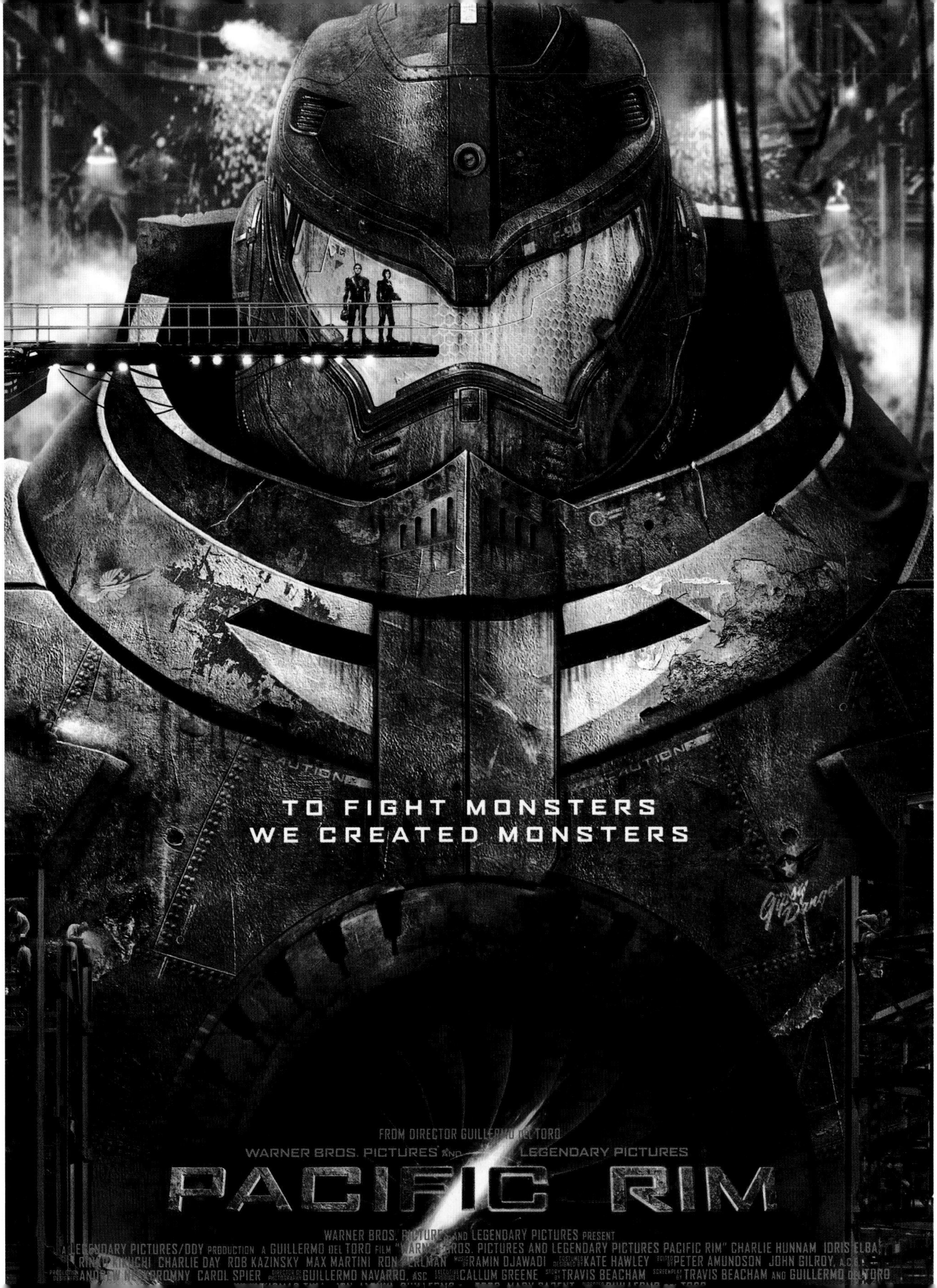

TO FIGHT MONSTERS
WE CREATED MONSTERS
WARNER BROS. PICTURES AND LEGENDARY PICTURES
PACIFIC RIM

Enlightenment, the so-called Age of Reason, there were no monsters. Beasts such as dragons were viewed as part of nature. With Frankenstein's creature, the *unnatural* was born. The chance to depict that forlorn and terrifying being for Universal was the equivalent of a Renaissance painter capturing the Crucifixion.

Throughout 2009 and 2010, countless drawings and sculptures honed the essential look of the creature. Del Toro wanted to escape the clichés of the past (no bolts, no spirit-levelled forehead), and draw close to Shelley's portrayal. The head needed to be that of a cadaver, the nose no more than a protruding bone. Doug Jones, who was due to be beneath the skin, spoke of 'a more emaciated' and 'pathetic looking creature'[9] but with unnatural physical prowess.

'You need to really *believe*,'[10] iterated del Toro.

'It's because he's a fanboy,' said Jones. 'He knows exactly how fanboys critique movies. He anticipates the "That wouldn't really work!" response.'[11]

Stepping back, it is hard to comprehend why Universal didn't go ahead with a faithful rendition of the classic by its most ardent disciple. But they vacillated on what to do with a catalogue of classic horror icons, trying blockbusters (*The Mummy*) and leaner modern reworkings (*The Invisible Man*), and del Toro's period piece fell between the cracks.

Besides, he had his own distractions.

In April 2008, a significant offer had wended its way to Bleak House from New Zealand. Peter Jackson was proposing del Toro as the ideal candidate to direct the (as was) two-part take on J.R.R. Tolkien's *The Hobbit* to serve as a prequel to his Oscar-wining version of *The Lord of the Rings*. Within the tale of Bilbo Baggins, who joins a gang of

quarrelsome dwarves on a quest to oust a dragon from their ancestral home, we will learn of how the great ring of power first came into the possession of this unassuming hobbit.

The portents were good. Jackson, wearying of Middle-earth management, was happy to pass on the baton, while he would still co-write and produce, alongside partners Philippa Boyens and Fran Walsh. New Zealand would again serve as

scenery. Del Toro was a proven master at delivering fantasy with conviction. Indeed, he and Jackson were kindred spirits: both were Ray Harryhausen obsessives; both began in the world of physical effects; both had prospered in Hollywood on their own terms; and each, being fervent collectors, had amassed a hoard of movie memorabilia.

'*The Hobbit* films? They are absolute quests,' delighted del Toro,

This would have been a Middle-earth entrained to a *Hellboy*-like eccentricity. The Dwarven realms came with great pipes, engines, and vast mechanical locks. He wanted to circumvent CGI for a more tactile universe, built as much on sets as out in the wild – with artificial forests that resembled Tolkien's original illustrations. Armour-plated trolls could roll into balls to skittle over foes. Dwarf chieftain Thorin's helmet would sprout antlers like the Elven king in *Hellboy II: The Golden Army*. The two films would pass through eight different, colour-coded seasons.

However, after nine months of intense groundwork (two years in total), del Toro abruptly departed New Zealand. With co-producers MGM struggling to resolve internal financial issues, the project had remained in a state of perpetual pre-production, and he could take no more.

Rumours flew like arrows through the forests of Hollywood. Had the del Toro and Jackson visions collided? Jackson insisted that he wanted 'Guillermo to have the freedom to do whatever he wanted.'[13] Del Toro hinted that there was 'discomfort'[14] over his intentions to fashion Smaug as a snake-like 'flying axe.'[15]

The truth was he could feel his career ebbing away in a billion-dollar pregnant pause. If and when the greenlight did arrive, six years of *Hobbit*-making still loomed ahead. He began to itch for more personal projects. The itchiest of all being his beloved adaptation of H.P. Lovecraft's *At the Mountains of Madness*, and Tom Cruise was showing interest.

Published in 1936, Lovecraft's novella recounts the events of a scientific expedition to Antarctica that stumbles across an ice-bound ancient city in an immense mountain range.

unable to resist the godfather of fantasy. 'There is absolutely no room for non-delivery.'[12]

He contemplated a fascinating balancing act, locating his films within Jackson's Middle-earth, while still flaunting his own stylistic tropes. Arguably, his directorial handwriting, with its orientation toward fairy tales, was better suited to the more whimsical, less galvanic tone of Tolkien's first novel.

Above: A Kaiju surfaces to attack the Sydney Opera House. While Guillermo del Toro wasn't keen on the cliché of demolishing global landmarks, he couldn't resist the mirror of Kaiju curves in the famous building.

What the scientists discover within draws them close to madness. This is the citadel of a long-dead race classified as Old Ones – vastly sophisticated creatures who fashioned the world, and us, eons ago. They came with huge tubular bodies, bat-like wings, and starfish-shaped heads. Tentacles were prominent. The story plugged into the greater Lovecraftian mythos, led by the totemic, many-tentacled god Cthulhu. The foolhardy scientists also learn that the Old Ones were (apparently) wiped out by their slave race, the shape-shifting Shoggoths. Below the ice, things begin to stir.

Del Toro's affinity with Lovecraft cannot be overstated. He wears a Miskatonic University alumni ring named for the author's fictional institution, and has read everything the reclusive Rhode Island writer ever set down on paper. All his films are infused with Lovecraft's arcane visions, and his statue, looking mildly perplexed, adorns Bleak House. *At the Mountains of Madness* was del Toro's grandest obsession, his magnum opus, what he half-jokingly referred to as his 'Sisyphean project.'[16] He first began to sketch ideas in his notebook in 1993.

Given a $100 million lottery win, del Toro once reflected, 'I would go about doing either *Mountains of Madness* or *Monte Cristo*. Those are the two films… Those are really very risky, very personal, very beautiful, very powerful things to do.'[17]

His script imposes an action-orientated plot upon Lovecraft's baroque descriptions, with his scientists caught between thawed-out races. The mood is *Alien* or John Carpenter's *The Thing* with a backdrop as immense as Middle-earth. A monster movie on the scale of David Lean, although – counter to del Toro's normal flow – the beasts were utterly malignant and unknowable.

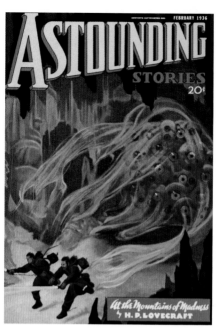

In 2006, he had tried to interest Warner Bros., but they were concerned about the pessimistic tone. There were no happy endings, no love story, no wisecracks. This was a fight for survival. He was pushing boundaries – $130 million for an R-rated horror movie that tore apart Judeo-Christian notions of creation with the stark news that humankind is the result of what del Toro dubbed a 'cosmic joke.'[18]

By 2010, returning from New Zealand, he had ammunition: not only Cruise's interest, but what he was now proposing to Universal, his next port of call, was the *Avatar* of horror movies, blooming with CGI, and James Cameron as producer.

Design work was underway at Cameron's Lightstorm Entertainment in Santa Monica, where the bountiful world of *Avatar* had been born. Sketches and notes already sprawled across del Toro's notebooks like the visions of a madman. Like Lovecraft, he used cephalopods – the soft-bodied class of octopuses, squids, and cuttlefish – as a biological building block.

Above left: The worlds of H.P. Lovecraft, with their extraordinary fauna and flora, have long cast a spell over Guillermo del Toro. Every one of his films feels the influence of the author.

Above right: An edition of *Astounding Stories* featuring Lovecraft's forbidding tale *At the Mountains of Madness* – with its exotic monsters and frozen setting, this was the tale that the director has striven to bring to the screen.

Opposite: Scientist Newton Geiszler (Charlie Day) prospects for vital data in unwholesome Kaiju remains – a regulation del Toro autopsy sequence that also plays humorously to a B-movie tradition.

The city itself, his most intricate labyrinth, would be specifically designed around the ergonomics of the creatures. He wanted the forbidding aura of Eastern filmmaking, where white symbolized death, and planned eight weeks of location shooting in Antarctica, or the nearest equivalent in Canada or Alaska.

He had never been 'more invested'[19] in a project, and when the blow came it was devastating.

They were a week away from crewing up. Early presentations had wowed executives, but another greenlight kept being delayed. Universal simply couldn't come to terms with the R-rating, and del Toro stood his ground. 'I think the R should be worn like a badge of merit in promoting the movie,'[20] he told them. Besides, it wasn't a gory movie so much as an intense movie. Unnerved, the studio demanded a compromise, and he mournfully withdrew from negotiations. 'Madness has gone dark,' he lamented. 'The 'R' did us in.'[21]

To add salt to deep wounds, a year later Ridley Scott's Alien prequel, the R-rated Prometheus, succeeded with an equivalent array of cosmic themes and biological horrors, right through to the revelation of our ungodly genesis. In Hollywood no one can hear you scream.

Before we abandon Lovecraft to his snowy grave, hope persists. Del Toro still wears his Miskatonic ring, promising he will until the film is made. 'They may bury me in it,'[22] he quipped. Fans have started pressuring Netflix, the adventurous, cash-rich streaming giant with whom he has recently forged a relationship on Pinocchio, to back a potential production.

Nonetheless, it was another turning point. 'The more you make plans, the more God laughs at you,'[23] he reported sourly. He simply couldn't go through years, even decades, filling his notebooks with false dawns. He badly needed to make a film.

In the summer of 2007, screenwriter Travis Beacham was strolling along Santa Monica Beach. He had rented an apartment nearby to get to grips with his first screenplay, the fantasy-themed murder mystery A Killing on Carnival Row, which had been optioned by del Toro. He

had come to love their uninhibited meetings. The director's lack of cynicism was infectious.

On this unseasonably cool morning, an otherworldly mist had rolled in off the Pacific, veiling the shoreline. Out beyond the metal bones of the Ferris wheel on Santa Monica Pier, Beacham imagined an astonishing sight: a giant robot locked in mortal combat with a colossal monster. 'These vast, godlike things,'[24] he recalled.

He turned the concept over in his mind for months. The robots, he decided, would be piloted by two humans, who were somehow psychically connected. But what would happen if one were killed? Even as monsters invaded from another dimension, it became a story of loss and recovery, and survivor's guilt. It had human dimensions.

Based on a twenty-five-page treatment entitled *Pacific Rim*, the ambitious production house Legendary acquired the project, sensing a potential franchise. By chance, days later, del Toro was meeting with Legendary. When they mentioned this high concept from his own protégé, his mind began to spin. Having first come onboard as producer, the loss of the Lovecraft changed everything. He decided to direct, urgent to get back on a set, urgent to prove he could deliver a blockbuster. In this case, one that literally busted entire blocks.

Left: Marketing materials for *Pacific Rim* revealing the three heroes: Stacker Pentecost (Idris Elba), Raleigh Becket (Charlie Hunnam), and Mako Mori (Rinko Kikuchi). And behind them the three hero Jaegers: Striker Eureka, Gipsy Danger, and Cherno Alpha.

It was the swiftest pre-production he had ever known. With *At the Mountains of Madness* felled on a Friday, he was at work on *Pacific Rim* the following Monday. Legendary brokered the deal, delivering a $190m budget and Warner Bros. to distribute. Had he the time, del Toro might have pondered the madness of Hollywood, where his great horror epic ran aground after years of development, and here he was with an even bigger budget and only outlines in his notebook. Featuring monsters the size of cathedrals fighting robots as tall as skyscrapers, *Pacific Rim* did at least offer the chance to decant some Lovecraftian monumentality into a living film.

More directly, *Pacific Rim* pays homage to the great Japanese *kaiju* (meaning 'strange beast') movies from the sixties and seventies, which matched an era of atomic paranoia with behemoths who demolished cities like piecrust. Of which, *Godzilla* was the prima dino-dona. 'I wanted *Pacific Rim* to be a real earnest, loving poem to the *kaiju* and *mecha* genre,'[25] announced del Toro. The *mecha* slant refers to a subdivision of Manga in which giant robots, steered by human heroes, fight off such gargantuan foes.

A phenomenon in Japan, the *mecha* series *Ultraman* told of a hero who secretly transforms into a giant alien clad in shining armour and spandex to defend a model Tokyo that comes up to his navel. It was imported to fill the afternoon slack on Mexican television – and no prizes for identifying the lonely blue-eyed boy who never missed an episode, and later staged stop-motion battles between his toys.

'These magnificent giant robots work on a mythical level,'[26] enthused del Toro, within whose mind the low-brow always jostles with the high. He christened his iron giants Jaegers after the German for 'hunter', and thought of Goya's painting *The Colossus*, in which a gigantic figure looms over a town (an allegory of invasion). He planned to infuse the hi-tech with the classical, harking back to the foundational tales of the Greeks with their Chimeras and Hydras. The last Jaeger depot, located in Hong Kong (China), is a giant, clanking citadel filled with machinery and backlit by flurries of hellish sparks like the great forges of the gods, or the roomy caverns planned for the dwarves of *The Hobbit*.

Honed over fifteen drafts, architecturally this is del Toro's most straightforward script. The fight against the Kaiju invaders has reached its culmination. With only three Jaegers still standing, apocalypse looms. Any hope of salvation lies in closing the inter-dimensional rift deep in the ocean that spawns the great beasts.

In close-up, we have the crews strapped into elaborate rigs housed in the Jaeger brains and known as Conn-Pods. Like deranged puppeteers, their human moves are synced to Jaeger moves: walking, grabbing, throwing

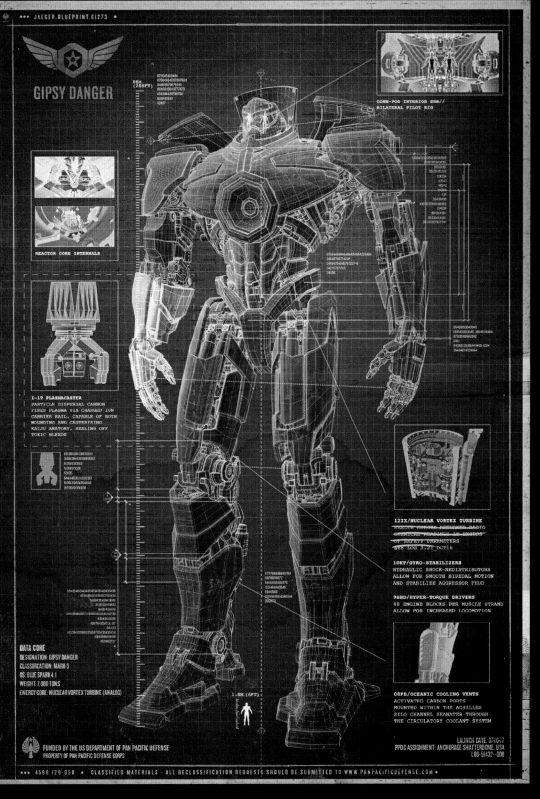

GIPSY DANGER

CONN-POD INTERIOR SRB//
BILATERAL PILOT RIG

REACTOR CORE INTERNALS

I-19 PLASMACASTER
PARTICLE DISPERSAL CANNON
FIRES PLASMA VIA CHARGED ION
CARRIER RAIL. CAPABLE OF BOTH
WOUNDING AND CAUTERIZING
KAIJU ANATOMY, SEALING OFF
TOXIC BLEEDS

12IX/NUCLEAR VORTEX TURBINE
~~HIGHER CHARGE DESIGNED PART~~
~~CHEMICAL READINGS IN ENGINE~~
~~OF SAFETY PARAMETERS~~
~~SEE LOG 3.21 OCT16~~

10KT/GYRO-STABILIZERS
HYDRAULIC SHOCK-REDISTRIBUTORS
ALLOW FOR SMOOTH BIPEDAL MOTION
AND STABILIZE AGGRESSOR FEUD

98BD/HYPER-TORQUE DRIVERS
40 ENGINE BLOCKS PER MUSCLE STRAND
ALLOW FOR INCREASED LOCOMOTION

DATA CORE
DESIGNATION: GIPSY DANGER
CLASSIFICATION: MARK-3
OS: BLUE SPARK 4.1
WEIGHT: 7,080 TONS
ENERGY CORE: NUCLEAR VORTEX TURBINE (ANALOG)

1.8M (6FT)

08FS/OCEANIC COOLING VENTS
ACTIVATED CARBON PORTS
MOUNTED WITHIN THE ACHILLES
SILO CHANNEL SEAWATER THROUGH
THE CIRCULATORY COOLANT SYSTEM

FUNDED BY THE US DEPARTMENT OF PAN PACIFIC DEFENSE
PROPERTY OF PAN PACIFIC DEFENSE CORPS

LAUNCH DATE: 07-10-17
PPDC ASSIGNMENT: ANCHORAGE SHATTERDOME, USA
L88-51432--008

Left: Fictional blueprints for the Jaeger Gispy Danger gives a sense of how the design wittily echoed the frames of superheroes and action stars.

Opposite above: A lethal Kaiju vents its fury. While Guillermo del Toro was keen to avoid any references to existing movie monsters, he encouraged his designers to look at real-world creatures for inspiration.

a hook or jab. It is a process known as *drift*, and they must partner up with someone who is 'drift compatible'[27] – a psychic connection that usually runs in the family.

Only now disillusioned maverick Raleigh Becket (Charlie Hunnam), who lost his brother to a Kaiju attack, must try and link with an outsider, Mako Mori (Rinko Kikuchi), a lethally talented but insecure orphan who saw her family perish beneath the dire footprint of Kaiju destruction in Tokyo. In a fairy-tale-style flashback, we see Mako as a tiny girl clutching a red shoe and pursued by a dragon, ash falling like snow as it had in Hiroshima. For del Toro, it was the central image.

'I thought of [*Pacific Rim*] as a Russian Doll, with a hurt girl at the centre, and then Mako, and then a giant twenty-five-storey robot. And finding that the strength came from the fact that at some point as a child she was afraid, and she's not afraid anymore. Which I think is essentially a metaphor for all of our lives, you know?'[28]

That the protagonists find a way to become drift compatible reflects the film's broader theme of human connection across barriers of culture, religion, sex, and language. The whole world was in the head of these robots, said del Toro. We can only save ourselves if we work together.

It is a tale told on a global level. We travel from Tokyo to Sydney to San Francisco to Vladivostok, while based in Hong Kong. This gives the film its title, and a near-future, neon-soaked cityscape that draws on *Blade Runner* and the great chaotic hubs of anime.

The cast is filled with quirky-cool, multi-cultural characters with splendid names. Idris Elba is Stacker Pentecost, the booming, one-dimensional commander of the Jaeger programme. Ron Perlman

lightens the mood as Hannibal Chau, a one-eyed black-market dealer in powdered Kaiju bones (prized as an aphrodisiac). Boffins Newton Geiszler (Charlie Day) and Hermann Gottlieb (Burn Gorman) dart about the plot, spit-balling exposition.

The story had what del Toro jokingly called 'complex simplicity.'[29] While a genre piece, underneath was a personal touch. 'I tried to articulate, not through one character, but through a choral structure, what it means to be human,' he grandly proposed. 'Each of those characters represents one virtue of being human: ingenuity, bravery, leadership.'[30]

The casting of Japanese star Kikuchi linked the film to its forebears, but she was also a striking, versatile actress who had featured in Alejandro González Iñárritu's *Babel*. She provides another solemn, big-eyed female presence at the heart of a del Toro film.

British art-student-turned-actor Hunnam had worked his way up to leading man via increasingly

prominent roles in *Cold Mountain, Green Street*, outlaw biker serial *Sons of Anarchy*, and Alfonso Cuarón's dystopian-themed drama *Children of Men*. The Mexican network still held strong. He had been up for Prince Nuada in *Hellboy II: The Golden Army*, but his cheekbones were deemed too strong for an elven exile. For the gung-ho pilot of a steeple-tall Jaeger they were ideal.

He may not look as good as Hunnam without his shirt, accepted del Toro, but the character was autobiographical. 'Raleigh has been out of a Jaeger for the same amount of time as I've been out of the directing chair! It wasn't exactly subtle, but it was really important for me. I'm getting back in the Jaeger.'[31]

Ironically, having finally resolved their financial bottleneck, *The Hobbit* films would go into production before *Pacific Rim*, but del Toro wasn't looking back. In November 2011, five years since he had last commanded a movie set, he was back beside his cameras.

Opposite: Flashback – while psychically linked, Charlie Hunnam's Raleigh Becket enters the memories of co-pilot Mako Mori, who, as a child (played by Mana Ashida) lost her family to a Kaiju attack.

Right: Burn Gorman as eccentric scientist Gottlieb, looking for a way of understanding their foe. Behind him are super-sized variations on the classic Guillermo del Toro foetus-in-a-jar motif.

Below: Raleigh piloting a Jaeger alongside his brother Yancy Becket (Diego Klattenhoff).

Left: With its epic, blockbusting scale, *Pacific Rim* was the biggest film Guillermo del Toro had ever made, but no less personal. As soon as he read the pitch, his mind returned to the Japanese *kaiju* monster films and *mecha* television series he had lapped up as a boy.

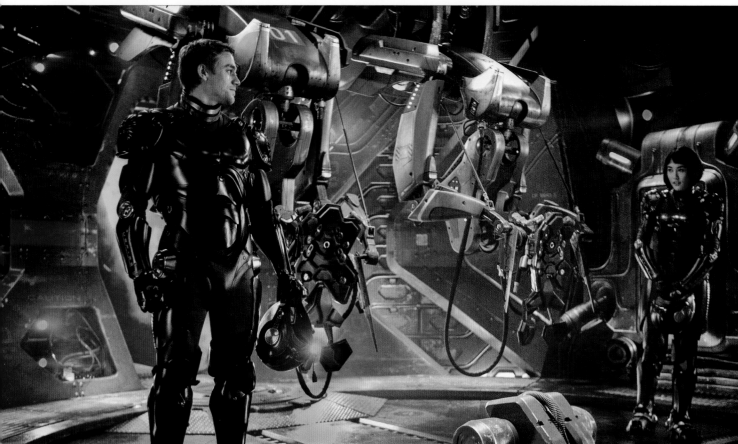

Above: Del Toro was thrilled to be back in his element, determined not to let himself overthink what was required. He actually finished ahead of schedule and underbudget.

Opposite above: Rinko Kikuchi's Mako Mori proves she has the moves to best new partner Raleigh Becket (Charlie Hunnam) – a brief reminder of the martial arts movies the director had mined for *Blade II*.

Opposite below: The partners prepare for launch. The cockpits or Conn-Pods were housed in the Jaegers' brain space, and built as gigantic multi-storey sets, rigged to hydraulics so the actors would feel every move their Jaeger made.

Even with over two thousand CGI shots, he was determined to run a very tight production. He had never shot a movie in less than 115 days, and now he would have just 103. He thought practically, scheduling a splinter unit so he could direct it first thing. He would work seventeen or eighteen hours a day, seven days a week. Those failed epics, *The Hobbit* and *At the Mountains of Madness*, were, he recognized, 'sort of gyms, training grounds'[32] for this movie.

The film spanned one hundred and one different sets across the huge spaces at Pinewood Studios in Toronto and out into two adjacent studios. The Conn-Pods were four storeys high and built on gimbals. Even behind the scenes it was a world only del Toro could concoct.

Indefatigable to the end, he barely left the set, as if it might prove to be an apparition. Cast and crew began to wonder if he ever slept. Without fail, they would find him at the video monitors, dealing with a million questions while nibbling on carrots

and hot sauce. He finished one day ahead of schedule and underbudget. He thought, 'this is the only shoot I have ever enjoyed.'[33]

Perlman had never known his old friend to be so specific in what he wanted. Yet del Toro resisted his usual 'ritual'[34] ballet between camera and character, allowing space for his actors to improvise. To a degree, they would shape how the Jaegers moved in the CGI wide shot, against packed city streets or knee deep in the ocean.

The three hero Jaegers, named Crimson Typhoon, Striker Eureka, and Gyspy Danger, are like giant knights in armour, wielding retractable swords and jet-propelled missiles, powered by a nuclear heartbeat. With big, armoured chests and tiny heads, they have the frames of eighties musclemen like Schwarzenegger and Stallone, but del Toro wanted them dented and scratched, literally beaten up. He extolled the 'language of World War II bombers… and huge oil tankers.'[35]

He and his team also looked at modern robot technology – remote-controlled machines to defuse bombs, military-grade stuff that gave them a trajectory of where the science might end up. He wanted a vein of photorealism to his outrageous plans. God was in the details. They showed how air was displaced as a Jaeger strode past an office block, warping the glass. Entire sets were rigged to hydraulics so that everything would jolt and bounce to a Kaiju footstep. The CGI models come enshrouded in a haze of particles from the debris of shattered buildings, or mist, or snow, or one of del Toro's classic downpours, replicated on set via gigantic plumbing.

Film Comment allowed that such evidently CGI scenes were 'possessed of real substance and weight.'[36] At its best, *Pacific Rim* was like a 'technologically souped-up George and the Dragon.'[37]

WARNER BROS. PICTURES AND   LEGENDARY PICTURES

PACIFIC RIM

ON JULY 12
GO BIG OR GO EXTINCT

The Kaijus are strange-looking dragons. Del Toro instituted a strict policy that neither beast nor robot would reference any pre-existing movie giant, but he was still infected with Lovecraft. The reptilian leviathans spill fluorescent blood and offer an array of horned heads, star-shaped jaws, and bizarre, angular body shapes. They also reflected real animals: the profile of a goblin shark, say, or the skin of an elephant. 'I asked my design team to just draw literally thousands and thousands of quick line drawings that were more silhouettes than detail, so they didn't get bogged down in the textures,'[38] he explained, determined not to get trapped in years of incremental development. They chose the shapes that were easy to read.

Only in the film's final throes do we get a glimpse of the insectoid civilization (a hint of the grand plan for *Mimic*) on the far side of the rift, and the why and how of Kaiju creation, but del Toro knew exactly why each looked that way.

Pacific Rim is a lot to take in. It brims with apocalyptic fury and mad invention. Like in *Blade II*, but on a monolithic scale, del Toro is back pursuing the juvenile kick of video games, taking out whatever residual frustrations remained from so many false starts by destroying entire cities.

For some critics it was an exuberant expression of his natural talents. 'Where the *Transformers* franchise has the soul-deadening effect of an extended toy infomercial,' appreciated *Slate*, '*Pacific Rim* offers at least some sense of watching an imagination at play.'[39] There is an initial rush in the headlong mêlées and mechanical mania, but it wears thin. The Vernean majesty becomes enslaved to the swarm-like excesses of CGI, leaving you to guess how one battle is won and another lost. It is harder to find the visual rhymes, the caress of magic. In career terms, *Pacific Rim* sees a director reasserting himself, flexing dormant muscles, and reminding Hollywood he could play the mainstream game. The

$410m worldwide (tallying especially well internationally) was enough to convince Legendary it was worth instigating a sequel. But del Toro's thoughts had turned to the roiling emotions of the gothic romance.

Above: *Pacific Rim* went on to become a global hit, kicking off a franchise, showing that Guillermo del Toro could succeed in the Hollywood playground without losing his personal touch.

The Others

Take a look into an alternative universe of del Toro's career and the films that haven't come to pass

Mephisto's Bridge
Based on the novel *Spanky* by Christopher Fowler, this is the story of a billboard designer who sells his soul to the Devil. 'It's my metaphor for my experiences in Hollywood,'[1] said del Toro.

An Honest Man
Written for Federico Luppi, this potential Spanish language film focuses on a meek accountant who murders his entire office to preserve his reputation.

The List of Seven
Sketches survive of a potential adaptation of Mark Frost's occult-themed murder mystery featuring Arthur Conan Doyle and Bram Stoker as protagonists.

The Coffin
This comic-book adaptation lies at a crossroads between *Cronos* and *Frankenstein*, with a brilliant scientist inventing a suit capable of housing a human soul – thus offering immortality, but as no more than a vapour. Rather like the ectoplasmic Johann Krauss from *Hellboy II: The Golden Army*.

Saturn and the End of Days
Smaller in scale, this whimsical tale follows a kid, Saturn, who witnesses the Rapture while walking to the supermarket.

Tarzan
Del Toro planned a characteristically brutal take on the loin-clothed hero. While still being a family movie, it would be set in a truly hostile environment. 'I want to portray how this guy becomes the toughest animal in the jungle,'[2] he said.

Pan
Here he planned an even more radical inversion of the standard telling. Imagine a Peter Pan wherein Hook is a grizzled detective on the trail of a child killer who might just be Peter.

The Lion, the Witch and the Wardrobe
An opportunity to adapt the C.S. Lewis classic was curtailed when del Toro let it be known he would prefer to forego the godlike lion Aslan's allegorical resurrection. And the appearance of Father Christmas.

The Wind in the Willows
For the Kenneth Grahame anthropomorphic classic, del Toro planned a mix of CGI and live action. But he bailed when Disney suggested giving Toad a skateboard.

Drood
Based on the Dan Simmons novel, here was a choice del Toro scenario in which the great nineteenth-century authors Wilkie Collins and Charles Dickens track a cult through a web of catacombs beneath London – with Collins's account of events rendered somewhat unreliable by his addiction to opium.

Justice League Dark
DC Comics offered a horror-aligned spin on the superhero team-up movie starring enticingly weird-looking anti-heroes like Swamp Thing and Deadman. It was to spread its tendrils into the DC-extended universe, alongside squares like Batman and Superman, but the studio wouldn't commit.

3993
The film originally planned to complete del Toro's Spanish Civil War trilogy following *The Devil's Backbone* and *Pan's Labyrinth*. It was to be set in both 1939 and 1993, with the re-opening of mass graves. Hence the title.

Above: With *Pan*, Guillermo del Toro wanted to turn tradition on its head.

FREAK HOUSE
Crimson Peak (2015)

How at long last he turned his peerless eye to the realms of gothic romance, filling the most extraordinary set of his or any career with emotions as wild as the frocks, and ghosts dripping in tragedy

What Guillermo del Toro loved about the Mexican movies of the fifties and sixties, the ones he had grown up with, was how they thought nothing of mixing genres. Horror stories came disguised as cowboy movies. Film noirs turned into romances. 'I probably inherited the licence to do the stream-of-consciousness approach to genre from Mexican cinema,' he reflected, 'the freedom where I can mix a Civil War with a fairy tale, you know?'[1]

The secret pleasure of del Toro's universe is that you're never sure where you stand. His ghost stories feel like Westerns; his extravagant superhero adventures have the aura of folktales; deep down, his vampire sagas are family dramas. The critic Kim Newman places his shapeshifting films under the umbrella term *'fantastique'*[2] (named after genre magazine and del Toro favourite, *Cinefantastique*) – a kind of mosaic of all the fantastical genres. The director's eighth film is literally built on shifting ground.

Right: The awe-inspiring interior set of the titular house was five storeys tall and fully three-dimensional.

At a glance, *Crimson Peak* is a haunted-house movie. Established traditions are honoured. A new arrival will confront the dire legacy bound to the walls of a great old nineteenth-century gothic pile. The pile in question is Allerdale Hall, which crowns a desolate hummock in what we are informed is Cumberland in northwest England. The arrival in question is that of sweet-natured American Edith Cushing (Mia Wasikowska), newly wed to the captivating Sir Thomas Sharpe (Tom Hiddleston), who resides in this daunting ancestral mausoleum with his icy sister Lucille (Jessica Chastain) and assorted members of the restless dead.

Naturally, haunted houses featured prominently on del Toro's to-do list. As a boy in Guadalajara, he would regularly break into abandoned houses in search of those left behind. Since his inaugural visit to Disneyland (an encounter with nirvana from which he has never fully regained his composure), his favourite attraction remains The Haunted Mansion. 'For some people, it's just a ride,' he said. 'For others like me, it's a way of life.'[3] In his collection, you'll find not only memorabilia, but also 'original artefacts'[4] from the ersatz mansion: props and models that have fallen out of use. The Bleak House features the same wallpaper and gargoyle sconces from the mansion's foyer.

At Comic-Con 2010, having returned from New Zealand empty-handed, he announced he was to direct an adaptation of the ghostly ride in the fashion of *Pirates of the Caribbean*. The plan was to tap into the 'core mythology'[5] of the Hatbox Ghost, a spectre in a top hat leaning on a cane and carrying a hatbox. Through a complex sequence of spotlights, his head would seem to vanish from his body and rematerialize in the box. According to legend, this proved *too* scary. With children led whimpering to the exits, the headless ghost was allegedly unplugged on the day the ride opened in 1969.

The more mundane truth is that the effect struggled against the ambient light, and was decommissioned a few months later. Del Toro worked his way through three different 'Hatbox' scripts, and talked Ryan Gosling into playing the lead role (they took a ride together to talk spooks). By which time Disney had re-embraced a more family-friendly ethos. Del Toro's vow to make children 'scream'[6] ended up decommissioned as well.

Crimson Peak actually pre-dated his clash with Disney ethics. It was written with longstanding collaborator Matthew Robbins in the wake of *Pan's Labyrinth* in 2006, when all things seemed possible. But then came the chance to make a second *Hellboy*, and those fallow years spent not making *The Hobbit*. Sold to Universal, the screenplay continued to gather dust when del Toro became occupied by *Pacific Rim*. Having developed a fruitful relationship wrestling monsters, *Pacific Rim* production company Legendary asked what he wanted to do next.

He showed them three scripts: those elusive marvels *At The Mountains of Madness* and *The Left Hand of Darkness*, and the more conservative (at least, in terms of budget) *Crimson Peak*. They went for the third option, joining up with Universal to back a still-not-inconsiderable 55-million-dollar costume drama set at the turn of the twentieth century.

'Ghosts are real, this much I know,'[7] breathes Edith, a woman of bright, modern thoughts drawn into an older, gloomier realm. It is the very first line, and it could easily be del Toro speaking. He knows ghosts to be real. Recall the tale of his dead uncle sighing from beyond the grave. While in New Zealand, scouting for *The Hobbit*, he stayed in a haunted hotel (he actively seeks them out). It

was off-season, so the place was empty. Even the manager had left for the night. The Overlook atmosphere was complete when, sat in bed, he heard a woman's agonized screams coming from a ventilation grille. Five minutes later came the heartbreaking sound of a man bawling. 'That was when I freaked out,' he admitted. 'I put on my headphones and watched the entire season of *The Wire* that I was carrying with me.'[8]

There is a temptation to read this as slightly tongue-in-cheek, but del Toro is being deadly earnest. His library boasts witness accounts that date back to the 1700s describing what he termed 'supernatural situations.'[9]

Onscreen, *The Devil's Backbone* revealed a gift for the icy poise of the classic ghost story, but that movie's

haunted orphanage is in stark contrast to the florid nightmare of *Crimson Peak*. Excess was now demanded. Where the former fed on the pancake-flat plains of the Spaghetti Western, the latter trips on the lurid vibe of that tribe of heated Italian horrors known as *gialli*, and more besides.

Even in del Toro's repertoire, the film's opening image is a striking one: Edith stranded in what H.P. Lovecraft might describe as the 'opalescent void'[10] (the director's yearning to adapt Lovecraft's tectonic fiction still bleeding into other projects), her parchment-pale features and nightdress sharply punctuated by splatters of *Hellboy*-red blood. Wind blows. Snow falls. Odd shapes leer out of the mist. She clutches a stained knife in a shaking hand. We sense this apparition,

living or dead, is the endgame toward which we are about to plunge through an opera of equally lavish imagery. Peak del Toro, if you will.

However, he would never call this a haunted-house movie, as such. For all those clanks and screeches ripping though the night (and day), all the phantoms shuffling along corridors, he billed his most audacious film as a 'Gothic Romance.'[11] Some clarification is required.

Experts cite the foundation stone of gothic literature as Horace Walpole's 1764 satirical novel *The Castle of Otranto*, which established the fixtures of a cursed family, a draughty castle, and inexplicable deaths. Significantly, the key exponents have been largely female: most famously, Ann Radcliffe (who went in for rational explanations for the supernatural in novels such as *The Mysteries of Udolpho*), Jane Austen (who parodied Radcliffe in *Northanger Abbey*), and the towering example set by Charlotte and Emily Brontë with their respective goth heavyweights *Jane Eyre* and *Wuthering Heights*. A rare male of the species is Henry James, with his seminal exercise in creepy children, *The Turn of the Screw*.

The next generation gave us the brilliant Daphne du Maurier, whose 1938 anti-romance *Rebecca* casts a long shadow over *Crimson Peak*. Note its slumbering mansion, Manderley; its dreamy atmospherics and psychological torments; and, in terms of plot structure, the confrontation between the innocent new love and the deranged housekeeper trapped in the past. Shirley Jackson's 1959 classic *The Haunting of Hill House* posited ambiguous psychic links between the house and its occupants.

Lines can also be drawn to the tradition of Latin American Gothic and magical realists like Gabriel García Márquez and Jorge Luis Borges (into

whose company del Toro is often placed). And to the recent successes of *Twilight* and *Fifty Shades of Grey*, which at least took themselves seriously. Indeed, *Crimson Peak* was part of a revival of the gothic tradition.

All of which had been bubbling away in the cauldron of del Toro's mind for years. Gothic Romance was another speciality of the house. Recall that the first film he saw at the cinema was William Wyler's 1939 take on *Wuthering Heights*. A little later, he discovered *Frankenstein* and *Jane Eyre*, and thought that both were 'emotional biographies of their authors.'[12] So began what he termed 'this immense spiritual love affair with the Brontës and Mary Shelley.'[13]

For the record: *Frankenstein* is more directly horror spliced with science fiction.

Del Toro would be the first to tell you that the Gothic Romance (and horror) sprang from the rich soil of the fairy tale.

Another key inspiration for *Crimson Peak*, he has said, is Sheridan Le Fanu's *Uncle Silas*, the 'perverse adventure'[14] of an adolescent girl Maud who goes to live with her wicked uncle, bringing to mind the struggles of *Cinderella*, *Snow White*, and *Pan's Labyrinth*.

'The rite of passage in gothic tales often requires the ambulation into a labyrinth of sorts, either the dark woods or a haunted edifice, or both,'[15] he explained, the critic mixing with the filmmaker.

Like the cracked heart of *Pan's Labyrinth*, *Crimson Peak* draws a deliberate distinction between two realities. Events begin in earnest amid the striving modernity of America, with its automobiles, printing presses and general aura of progress, before pivoting to England, which appears trapped beneath a veil of fantasy. 'If I had to vote for the most haunted country in the world, I'd vote for England,'[16] laughed del Toro. We travel with Edith from life into genre. Even

Above: Interior decline – a great, decaying mansion was the defining setting for the Gothic Romance, and Guillermo del Toro produced the definitive article.

Opposite: Joan Fontaine's heroine withstands the glare of Orson Welles' Mr. Rochester in the classic 1943 adaptation of *Jane Eyre*, one of a host of classics that served as inspiration for *Crimson Peak*.

Thomas's clever inventions struggle to find purchase in the clogged earth. A dreamer, he has fashioned dinosaur-like contraptions to extract the precious clay that has rendered the soil a sickly shade of red. The house perches uneasily on this sludgy midden that spews to the surface, leaving great bloodstains on the landscape.

What distinguishes del Toro, claimed film historian David Thomson, 'is the strength of the literary structure of his material.'[17] And *Crimson Peak* finds him at his most determinedly novelistic. In the opening credits, the title comes embroidered on the cover of an old hardback.

Then again, there are as many film references as bookish ones. Gothic Romance has thrived in cinema. Buñuel made a version of *Wuthering Heights*. Hitchcock made the definitive, Oscar-winning adaptation of *Rebecca*, billowing with melodrama. At the movies, gothic teeters on the edge of absurdity.

Through the 1960s, Roger Corman conjured up his Edgar Allan Poe cycle, with Vincent Price, that virtuoso of ham, presiding over doom-laden families holed up within gothic ramparts. Each one, be it *The Fall of the House of Usher*, *The Raven* or *The Pit and the Pendulum*, was delivered in throbbing Technicolor more psychedelic than medieval. Not to forgo Price in Joseph L. Mankiewicz's fulsome 1946 serving of inexplicable deaths and troubled real estate, *Dragonwyck*. Or the sight of newlywed Ingrid Bergman being driven mad by Charles Boyer in *Gaslight*, which is the origin of the term 'gaslighting'. Or *Bluebeard*, in which Richard Burton's aristocrat works his way through a flock of beautiful wives, concealing their frozen bodies in a castle vault as an alternative to divorce.

While reclaiming the power of such melodrama, del Toro was again subverting the rules from within. He called it 'recontexualization.'[18] One Mexican boot was still firmly in the camp of horror. These are genuine ghosts, not metaphors or delusions. The tone is scary, the themes deep and heartfelt. 'It's the first time I've tried to marry the *Pan's Labyrinth* and *Devil's Backbone* sensibilities with a larger cast and larger budget,'[19] he said. Plot, character, costume, production design, music, sound, and, uppermost, the great cathedral set of Allerdale Hall are entwined like a tank of eels.

With her industrialist father (Jim Beaver) savagely murdered, his crushed skull laid bare in the *de rigeur* morgue scene, Edith is now heiress to a fortune. Inducted into the gloomy confines of Allerdale, she soon suspects that the Sharpes are strapped for funds. Thomas becomes distant, Lucille dangerous, and from the very first night, the dead commence their attempts to issue a warning. Like Santi, the lost soul in *The Devil's Backbone*, the writhing spirits prove to be less phantoms than witnesses for the prosecution.

The kernel of *Crimson Peak*, emphasized co-screenwriter Robbins, was the notion that the protagonist could form a 'strange alliance with the very creatures that were initially so frightening.'[20] The writers wanted to see if they could create a movie in which our expectations about a ghost story were violated. The monsters, del Toro enjoyed telling journalists, were once again of the human variety. Edith must try to decipher the riddles of the undead in order to save herself.

Given that for much of the time the story encircles the central trio

of brother-sister-prey, with Charlie Hunnam's overlooked paramour orbiting at a distance, casting would always set a conspicuous tone. It proved a tricky business. Initially, Benedict Cumberbatch and Emma Stone had been announced as Thomas and Edith, with Jessica Chastain confirmed as Lucille. While producing *Mama*, which featured Chastain, del Toro had shown her the script, thinking of the red-headed star as Edith. She surprised him by pushing to play Lucille instead, relishing the challenge: as well as conveying barely contained emotional storms, she had to learn the piano. Then, as production delays jammed up the start date, he lost Stone to an incoming production and Cumberbatch to an amicable if perplexing change of heart.

Wise now to Hollywood's changeable weather patterns, del Toro re-orientated his thinking. 'I always tell my wife, "If you want to furnish a room, you start by buying a key piece of the furnishings, and then that's your anchor. Then you decorate around that."'[21] The first anchor in his cast had been Cumberbatch. After he departed, del Toro used Chastain as his fixed point, which presented new ideas for Thomas and eventually Edith too. 'Tom Hiddleston struck me as a really good balance to Jessica's strengths,' he mused. 'Then Mia struck me as a really good counterpart. She has a very different, much more quiet, deeply centred strength to Jessica.'[22] It wasn't about their talent or bankability, it was about chemistry.

Left: The new flame - Thomas Sharpe (Tom Hiddleston) woos wealthy heiress Edith (Mia Wasikowska) by skilfully keeping a candle alight through their waltz.

Chastain was from Sacramento in California, and best known for modern hits like *Zero Dark Thirty* and *Interstellar*, though her pale skin was positively Victorian. The London-born, Eton-educated Hiddleston was cut from old theatrical cloth (his delivery was as crisp as a heel on stone), but his recent run as Loki in the *Thor* films had revealed a flash of charming villainy. The ethereal Wasikowska, an Australian, came with fitting baggage, having taken the leads in both *Alice in Wonderland* and *Jane Eyre*.

The early gothic tales, said del Toro, 'require an innocent or "pure" protagonist at the centre in order to function.'[23] He used oversized props to emphasize the vulnerability of his heroine, a trick borrowed from Hitchcock's *Rebecca*. Nevertheless, Edith is no damsel in distress. She is both naïve and enlightened. A product of the inquisitive, literary side of del Toro's personality, she is a prospective writer, keen to tell ghost stories (and pertinently not love stories), still haunted by her childhood encounter

with a cadaverous mother with bones as black and glossy as an oil slick.

None of the characters is exactly archetypal. Lucille has an ocean of passion and bitterness beneath the icecap of her soul. Her feelings toward her brother fall under the heading of unhealthy, but are very real. Behind her scowl lie another dead mother (but by no means gone), and a stint in an asylum. She joins ranks with those warped souls Jacinto, Vidal, and scheming Prince Nuada from *Hellboy II: The Golden Army*. The damaged children of del Toro's universe.

Like *Pan's Labyrinth*, *Crimson Peak* is a film driven by female energy. Hiddleston's Thomas grows more and more passive as the film goes on – finally to take his place as a ghost, his ashen forehead cracked open like Jesús Gris in *Cronos*, Santi in *The Devil's Backbone*, or the shell of a boiled egg. Hunnam's Dr. Alan is a red herring in a grey suit. Everything points toward his arrival in the nick of time, only for his heroic trajectory to be rudely interrupted by a knife to the armpit

(Jacinto suffers the same intimate wound in *The Devil's Backbone*), leaving him in dire need of rescue.

Filming through the spring of 2014, del Toro was clearly having a ball. He would regularly break out in song to serenade his crew. Every few weeks, a mariachi band was invited to perform during lunch. He had held back revealing the house to his actors until it was ready, delighting in their awestruck expressions; and as with *Pacific Rim* was more open to improvisation than he had ever been before. Lucille furiously slamming the pot of porridge down on the breakfast table then scooping up the mess with her bare hands was entirely of Chastain's making, a stray glimpse of her mania. At times, it was like a stage play.

Edith and Lucille are duelling for supremacy in these Freudian corridors like Sigourney Weaver and her alien – though with less acid for blood than acid for tea, as Lucille concocts unpalatable brews, and Edith's declining health is mirrored in the thinning weave of her gowns. You can argue that Edith is a play on the 'final girl' trope from slasher movies. The only nudity on show is male. By the standards of modern Hollywood this was feminist stuff, and enough to give the studio pause (it was another reason why the film took eight years to get made). But del Toro has been in the company of strong women his entire life: wives, daughters, grandmothers, all those spellbinding female authors who constantly whisper in his ear. 'Whenever a female writer has tackled [a Gothic Romance],' he said, 'these tales typically become intelligent, complex, and empowering.'[24]

He didn't think of it as political so much as good storytelling. 'If you go back to *Cronos*, it's a two-hander between two figures that in 1991, when I made *Cronos*, were always marginal in narrative. One is an old male, and a young female. I have more interest in figures that you normally don't get to see centred in a genre narrative, it makes it so much more interesting for me.'[25]

The other monster of *Crimson Peak* is the house itself. Del Toro wanted the Sharpes' shambolic domain to feel 'a little bit like an organism.'[26] When air funnels down the chimney, enraging the fire, the whole place seems to be breathing. Thanks to a gaping wound in the roof, snow falls into the vast atrium (a nod to the snow-globe kingdom of Xanadu in *Citizen Kane*). This is gothic architecture out of control like an infection. The place is rotting from the top down. For del Toro, the house has gone mad.

Right: Determined to redefine the movie ghost, Guillermo del Toro depicted his jerking, agonised undead in a violent red with CGI enhancements.

Designed using architectural software, the vast interior was literally carved by hand out of durable foam by Tom Sanders (who had girded his gothic on *Bram Stoker's Dracula*). However versatile CGI had proved on *Pacific Rim*, del Toro's haunted house had to be real. That was sacrosanct. This was his twisted elaboration on the famous Disney attraction, and was built in all its terrible majesty on the same vast soundstages of Pinewood Studios in Toronto that had housed his gigantic Jaegers. They offered ample space for this groaning interior, five storeys tall and fully three-dimensional. He was still thinking big.

In a sense, Bleak House had become a movie. He built its spirit into this great edifice crumbling beneath the weight of references. Tom's room reveals intricate automatons and clockwork dolls: porcelain eyeballs lie in trays, and eerie dummies stare from the corners. The library has original copies. The severe portrait of the Sharpes' dowager mother, done in the style of Sargent or Whistler (del Toro's grandmother might just

be the model), was commissioned seven months in advance in order for it to look genuinely aged. Every detail counted. There was a working elevator that connected three floors for that touch of the mechanical in del Toro's antique tableaux.

Allerdale Hall is an exaggeration but never a parody of the great houses of movie history, where his camera could prowl like those that had roamed the labyrinthine worlds of *The Innocents*, *The Haunting* – and *The Shining*, that 'Mount Everest of haunted-house movies.'[27] And there is a touch of Ridley Scott's other great genre pieces *Legend* and *Blade Runner*, with their dense, romantic, weather-worn backdrops.

When devising the layout of his sets, del Toro always keeps his cinematographer in mind. There must be room for the camera to move, and take the audience on the ride. In this case, he brought in Dan Laustsen, who had been by his side in the noir-like underworld of *Mimic*. They didn't hold back. Lighting through the windows from the outside gave the ambience a crepuscular, painterly

glow. The bold swathes of colour in the sets, from blacks to reds to teal and turquoise to whiteouts, are in honour of Mario Bava.

That shy Italian master, godfather of *giallo*, was another enormous influence on del Toro. Like del Toro, Bava served his apprenticeship in special effects and believed in the potency of genre. Through the 1960s, he developed an exquisite form of gothic via a suite of cult horrors made in carnivalesque style. 'Every decision he makes in terms of colour, saturation, composition, or lighting feeds into the story,'[28] appreciated del Toro. Even the title, *Crimson Peak*, feels like it's paying homage to the blazing reds of *Kill, Baby... Kill!*, the tale of a vengeful ghost of a murdered girl in late nineteenth-century Transylvania. As del Toro saw it, Bava's elevated visuals create a kind of habitat that allows the supernatural manifestations to exist.

Del Toro's ghosts all come lacquered in scarlet from the clay in which their bodies were concealed. No one had ever seen red ghosts before, he reasoned. They also had to be real. Which meant slender actors in hideous, twisted costumes, including the ever-versatile and ever-willing Doug Jones. Any CGI was for cosmetic enhancement. Their contorted features reflect their emotional torment: jaws are displaced, skulls broken, skin sags from bones (rather like The Pale Man), and mouths yawn beyond possibility. Del Toro had a backstory for every one of them.

Having the dead on set brought an immediacy to the lead performances. They didn't have to imagine what was there. The juddering, bone-grinding effort it takes to move after the onset of rigor mortis was choreographed like dance steps. The ghosts could interact with their environment. The wretch that rises out of the floor actually 'came out of a trench,' recalled del Toro: 'we then added the floor on top.'[29]

Smothering is a theme. Lucille's version of love is a suffocating devotion. 'A monstrous love makes monsters of all,'[30] she whispers, insinuating that the Sharpe state of mind is a hand-me-down psychosis. The entire film is smothered in symbolism. That oily clay, which wells up between floorboards, is the vivid representation of the blood money upon which the house is held up.

The insects of choice are butterflies and their night-time siblings, moths. The winged motif is repeated endlessly across props and sets like a challenge to viewers to keep returning. The costumes are extensions of both décor and character. Dressed in voluminous golden dresses that pop like sunlight out of the inky darkness, Edith is the butterfly. Lucille is the moth: her teal gowns, as tight as armour, blend into the wallpaper like the real moths that fester in the gloom. With his whole Dickensian undertaker chic, Thomas looks like he has wondered in from the wrong era entirely.

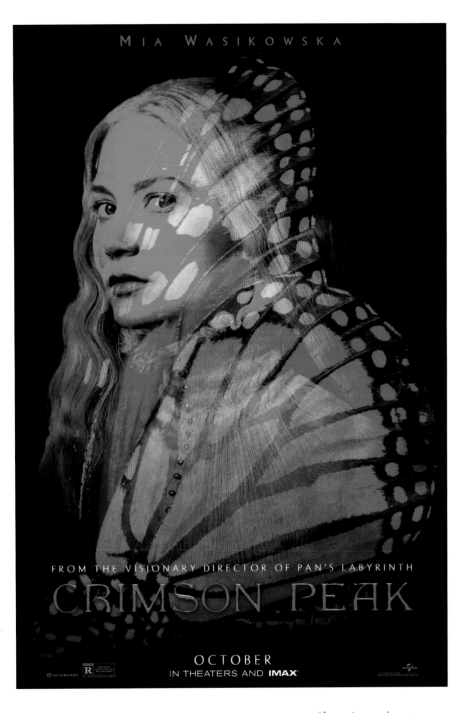

MIA WASIKOWSKA

FROM THE VISIONARY DIRECTOR OF PAN'S LABYRINTH

CRIMSON PEAK

OCTOBER
IN THEATERS AND IMAX

Above: A surreal poster centred on a perturbed Edith (Mia Wasikowska). Del Toro was determined that he was making a Gothic Romance and not a horror movie.

Above: Guillermo del Toro
liked to think of Allerdale Hall
as a house that had gone mad
– the very fittings coming
apart as the awful history of
its occupants is revealed.

Above: However horrific, all of Guillermo del Toro's images are equally beautiful. Case in point: the scarlet ghost of the Sharpe siblings' mother is framed against the oxidized green of the bathroom walls.

Left: Still life – the artist-director poses his leading lady in rapturous dandelion, against the naturalistic light pouring in through the window.

'What I enjoy is presenting the absolutely horrible in the most beautiful way,' del Toro concluded. 'I love it when beauty is disrupted by violence. I cannot say why, it's just a mixture I'm attracted to.'[31]

Amid mounting excitement and a spectacular slew of trailers, *Crimson Peak* left fans wondering if there was such a thing as too much del Toro. The global box office tally of $75 million was perceived as a disappointment (especially the lacklustre $31 million it earned in America). It is a sumptuous piece that presents a conundrum – can a film be too beautiful? For once, was the dish too rich? 'Del Toro won't let a scene pass without smashing the audience in the face with it, but you can't help but admire his audacity,'[32] sighed an exhausted *Atlantic* magazine.

Compared to the elegant balance between story and style achieved in *Pan's Labyrinth*, *Crimson Peak* is overcome by raptures. The drama never reaches the frenzy of the furniture. There is simply not enough story to bear the weight of the macabre imagery. 'If you're a keen enough viewer, there are no twists – or, at least, the incestuous, murderous couple at the film's heart won't really come as a surprise to you,'[33] said *Film Comment*. When the Sharpes' skulduggery is finally exposed, motives revealed, and comeuppance meted out, the feeling is certainly anti-climactic.

Still, you can't help but agree, with *The Nation*, that 'film culture would be much poorer if it looked away from this deliciously mordant work by del Toro, one of the few writer-directors today who doesn't just craft images but thinks in them.'[34]

And del Toro showed no signs of losing his train of thought. He was already set on another adult blend of genres seasoned with the gothic. Only now the monster was going to be the romantic lead.

THE LOVE AQUATIC
The Shape of Water (2017)

How a naturally bizarre and deeply felt love story between a mute janitor, and an amphibious man held captive in a military base, swept the Academy Awards off their feet. Any political implications were entirely deliberate

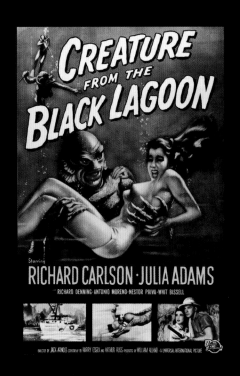

Above: An original poster for the 1954 B-movie that took root in Guillermo del Toro's imagination from the moment he saw it as a boy.

Right: The net result – a director's reworking of one of his favourite monster movies into a lyrical inter-species romance like no other.

'**I** am an immigrant,'[1] declared Guillermo del Toro pointedly, his tuxedo punctuated with an aquamarine handkerchief, the Academy Award for Best Director clutched tightly in his right hand. What he so loved about movies, he wanted to make clear from the podium of the Dolby Theatre on Hollywood Boulevard, was that they erased lines in the sand. Art brings people together.

It was 4 March 2018, and he was having the night of his life. His latest film, his tenth, would walk away with four Oscars: Best Score, Best Production Design, and the crowning one-two of Best Director and Best Picture. No one was missing the fact that *The Shape of Water*, despite being set in 1962, was a telling riposte to a contemporary America that had lurched to the right politically, with the White House spewing a monstrous rhetoric of division along with hot-headed plans to build a wall along its Southern border.

Receiving the Best Picture award a little later, del Toro picked up where he had left off. He spoke of growing up in Mexico watching movies from all over the world. Multicultural forces had shaped his films. A sensation by any measure, his latest, *The Shape of Water*, was on its way to making $195 million around the world, accompanied by rapturous reviews, and now Hollywood's ultimate benediction – Academy Awards.

Del Toro finished by reiterating his most fundamental belief – that fantasy was the perfect tool with which to address real-world issues. 'This is a door,' he impressed upon his peers. 'Kick it open and come on in.'[2]

Generous as the invitation was, this was a victory for a unique filmmaking alchemy. Who else would think to frame a political allegory around the romance between a mute janitor and an amphibian man, as loosely based on a B-movie that hadn't greatly troubled the Oscars in 1954?

When del Toro first saw *Creature from the Black Lagoon* he didn't react as other people did. He didn't scream or hide his eyes. He didn't laugh at the ageing special effects and corny dialogue, or denounce the obvious Californian locations. Instead, he found himself entranced by the underwater scenes, groundbreaking for their day, in which stunt diver Ricou Browning's 'Gill-man' swam beneath actress Julie Adams. There was a grace to his movements that spoke of a strange desire. The romantically inclined six-year-old from Guadalajara found himself yearning for the terrifying prehistoric creature, discovered on a geology expedition deep into the Amazonian jungle, to end up with the girl.

'I loved that the creature was in love with her,' he recalled wistfully, 'and I felt an almost existential desire

for them to end up together. Of course it didn't happen.'[3]

Jack Arnold's creature feature, in the original 3D, was another metamorphic moment in del Toro's life. Alongside *Duel* and *Blade Runner*, he must have watched it more than any other film. The creature design was the most beautiful he had ever seen. In precise and passionate detail, he could relate the terrible injustice suffered by the suit's true designer, Milicent Patrick, who had her credit stolen by make-up artist Bud Westmore. One of the many pleasures offered by the *Hellboy* universe was the chance to portray Abe Sapien, best described as a classically educated Gill-man.

In his thirties, making headway in Hollywood, del Toro had pitched a remake to Universal on several occasions. One idea, he said, was to set it in the era of Victorian exploration, 'with a balloon and steam riverboats.'[4] Very him. Whichever period they decided was commercially viable, he insisted on telling the story from the creature's perspective. 'They didn't go

for that,'[5] he laughed, contemplating yet another pitch that sounded like the ramblings of a desert hermit to studio ears. 'I said, "I think they should end up together." They didn't go for that, either.'[6]

Wearying of the endless back-and-forth, del Toro locked it away in his cabinet of unfulfilled dreams. That was until 2011, when he was sitting down to breakfast with Daniel Kraus, who was to be a co-writer on his television series *Trollhunters*. They were lightly tossing ideas around, when Kraus mentioned a story he was working on about a janitor at a secret government facility who discovers a supernatural creature and manages to smuggle it home. At that moment, all of del Toro's love for the Gill-man flooded back into his heart, and he saw a new way of telling a love story. He made a deal on the spot to buy Kraus's idea and started on the screenplay.

He had flirted with interspecies (or inter-reality) ardour in the *Hellboy* films, with the tangled relationship between Liz and Red. And explored the bond between the living and the dead in *Crimson Peak*. There is an unmissable sexual charge to the purring Faun in *Pan's Labyrinth*. This, however, was to be a love story in the grand, melodramatic Hollywood tradition. Albeit between a human and a sentient fish.

So it wasn't a remake of *Creature from the Black Lagoon* so much as homage, instilled with the spirit of B-movies (as most of his films are, of course) and weepies, and made with enough elegance and daring to make it an awards contender. He envisaged the janitor as a mute and lonely woman named Elisa (unusually but vividly cast in the shape of British actress Sally Hawkins), all but invisible in her job at a military research laboratory in Baltimore. Here she witnesses the arrival of their cruel secret – an amphibious humanoid (Doug Jones, naturally), hauled far from his Amazonian home and subjected to vile experiments led by the sadistic Colonel Strickland (Michael Shannon). One look in the creature's blue-black eyes and it is love.

WINNER VENICE · TELLURIDE · TORONTO · BFI LONDON

A GUILLERMO DEL TORO FILM

THE SHAPE OF WATER

DIRECTED BY
GUILLERMO DEL TORO

SCREENPLAY BY
GUILLERMO DEL TORO & VANESSA TAYLOR

STORY BY
GUILLERMO DEL TORO

Though set far from Spain and its shadowy history – the location for *The Devil's Backbone* and *Pan's Labyrinth* – *The Shape of Water* explores similar themes of social intolerance. More than ever, del Toro was motivated by the growing divisions defining his own times: 'The idea that ideology is separating all of us, more and more, in the most intimate spaces.'[7] The rescue operation will unite a collection of disparate outcasts: not only the amphibian and voiceless Elisa, but her only friends, African-American work colleague Zelda (Octavia Spencer) and insular gay neighbour Giles (Richard Jenkins).

'I've always believed that by creating visuals and ideas, you can take what is fantasy and make it truth,' said del Toro, bringing rich expression to the central tenet of his career. 'You can make movies that are truthful and that deal with the fantastic as a parable.'[8]

As a child, coerced by his grandmother into church (where naturally he preferred the gargoyles to the solemn statues of saints), he only ever tuned into a sermon if it concerned the parables. They were stories filled with metaphors and double meanings, stories that illuminated the world. He thought of them as a Biblical spin on fairy tales. They were stories that had soul.

Elisa is hardly a paragon of virtue. She is a grown woman. Each morning she sets eggs to boil on her stove, before scurrying to the bath to masturbate. Whatever subtext lurked beneath the surface of the Black Lagoon is made abundantly clear. This is del Toro at his most whimsical and shapeshifting, which is saying a lot for a director who once staged a skirmish between a sunburn-red demon and a giant orchid. It is also del Toro at his most erotic.

Such were the plans he put before Fox Searchlight, the arthouse-orientated studio arm that had taken good care of idiosyncratic filmmakers such as Wes Anderson, Darren Aronofsky, and Noah Baumbach. He was armed with drawings and models, and he read out parts of the script. Ready as ever with the hard sell.

'At the end of the pitch,' he said, 'everybody was crying.'[9]

So he pushed a little harder. How would they feel if he shot it in black and white to match his memories of that 1954 cult classic? There were some telling looks: if he was insistent on black and white then the budget would be $16.5 million. 'And how much if it is in colour?'[10] he enquired. The answer was $19.5 million.

'Colour it is,'[11] he agreed.

That said, he bade cinematographer Dan Laustsen to shoot in a near monochromatic symphony of greens from algae to brine to the radioactive-rich filling of a Key lime pie. In a visual rhyme going back to *Cronos*, the only red we see is blood, and the coat and shoes that Elisa dons post-coitally.

Within certain parameters, del Toro was keen to keep things small. To use the limitations to push himself as he had on *Pan's Labyrinth*, and drawing inspiration from Searchlight stable-mate and old friend Alejandro González Iñárritu's recent Oscar-winning oddity *Birdman or (The Unexpected Virtue of Ignorance)*, which had stretched a minimal budget in imaginative directions. In a watershed period for Mexican cinema, within three years the Three Amigos will each win an Oscar for Best Director. Alfonso Cuarón, would pick up his for the more expansive magic of *Gravity*.

Del Toro has a typically colourful metaphor for the burden of the plump studio movie. It is like adopting 'a baby tiger,'[12] he said. Adorable at first, but they soon grow up and want to eat you. A bigger budget allows big ideas to bloom, but leads inevitably to the broadest possible marketing campaigns. It broke his heart that *Crimson Peak*, which had cost $55 million, had been vociferously sold as a straight horror movie, something he suspected had contributed to its financial failure.

Opposite: The sadistic Colonel Strickland (Michael Shannon), who runs the base, is the film's equivalent of Guillermo del Toro's tidy fascists.

Below: During her break, Elisa (Sally Hawkins) plays music to soothe the mysterious creature confined to the base. Notice how the director unites the colour scheme of the walls with the costume.

With Searchlight giving him freedom to make modestly priced but sophisticated fables without oversight, del Toro had, at last, found a steady platform for his filmmaking. Indeed, it is unclear if he will ever return to the blockbusting arena, with all its bruising pressures. It is telling that he stepped away from directing an immediate sequel to *Pacific Rim* (serving only as producer on the underwhelming *Pacific Rim: Uprising* in 2018) when the production shifted to Australia from his regular haunt of Pinewood's Toronto studios.

With the enormous stages of Pinewood booked up, *The Shape of Water* had to adapt to Toronto's relatively compact Cinespace Studios, which was between seasons of the del Toro-produced vampire series *The Strain*. A joyous shoot ran from August to November 2016.

Del Toro has never orientated his career by the Hollywood north of financial gain. 'You need to define success by the degree of fulfilment,'[13] he insisted. He never reads the trades. He couldn't name the hot executives. He knows nothing of the current trends; the inevitable sequels. 'When I was growing up,' he said, 'we founded a cinema club that become the Guadalajara Film Festivals, and we would create programs to show the films of Max Ophüls or Preston Sturges. I was the projectionist, the ticket seller, and the moderator. It was about *film*.'[14]

The Shape of Water inhabits a border country where realism and surrealism meet. Named after the flower girl in *Pygmalion* and its musical iteration *My Fair Lady*, Elisa lives above the antique Orpheum picture palace. Threads of light from the cinema screen below find their way up through her patchwork floorboards, and a giddy director took the chance to experiment with a musical number in which Elisa dreams of herself spinning across a ballroom with her webbed partner in top hat and tails – mirroring Fred Astaire and Ginger Rogers in *Follow the Fleet*.

Movies are the new fairy tales. Del Toro referred to *The Shape of Water* as a 'love letter'[15] to the great pageant of Hollywood history in all its grandeur

Douglas Sirk's lush and sentimental portraits of postwar America. We catch glimpses of lost favourites like the Biblical epic *The Story of Ruth* and the musical *Mardi Gras* playing at the Orpheum, and Shirley Temple movies on Giles's TV set.

The Shape of Water is the culmination of the director's kaleidoscopic approach to genres. Or 'genre-fluid,'[16] as the *New Yorker's* Anthony Lane dubbed the malleable approach. Del Toro, he added, 'delivers a horror-monster-musical-jailbreak-period-spy-romance. It comes garnished with shady Russians, a shot of racial politics (Strickland talks to Zelda about "your people," meaning African-Americans), puddles of blood, and a healthy feminist impatience

Above: In tribute to the sentiment of Hollywood's Golden Era, Guillermo del Toro had old melodramas playing on television screens and in the picture house below the apartments.

Opposite: Even for del Toro, *The Shape of Water* is a highly stylized film, with the aquamarine colour spilling from the wallpaper to the egg cartons, punctuated by bursts of red - seen here in the packets of salt.

The array of tones is startling. Del Toro confidently steers his film between comedy, cruelty, paranoia, the overtly political, the deeply romantic, and the undeniably mystical.

Yes, it was made in the English language (as well as sign language and a chorus of amphibian shrieks). And yes, it is set in America, filmed in Canada, and has the Cold War as a backdrop. Nonetheless, after *3993* was abandoned, it is *The Shape of Water* that completes the trilogy of political fables with *The Devil's Backbone* and *Pan's Labyrinth*. They are the films that are the most personal, cathartic expression of his storytelling.

During the long hours of promotion, when he would always give so much more of himself than other directors, he mused that these films were a form of therapy. 'Completely, fully, one hundred percent therapy for me. How they played for other people, or whether they played and are seen as beautiful fantasy or this or that, I have no control over.'[18]

If *The Shape of Water* had flopped, he told a Mexican television station, he would have considered retiring from directing.

This one was more artistically complex, the metaphors more deeply embedded. This was the first time

in his career he took a step back to consider exactly what kind of emotional response he was looking for.

Elisa's crumbling apartment is mottled with water stains. The walls are a smudged aquamarine. Holes in the ceiling let in the rain. Light dances in the air. Barely distinguishable on one wall is a mural of *The Great Wave off Kanagawa,* the legendary Japanese woodblock print by Katsushika Hokusai (a key motif in *Pacific Rim*). The cracks look like tributaries. The place feels submerged in dream. Especially compared to the lifeless, pre-fab functionality of Strickland's home.

The wellspring of childhood memories was ever-present. The ecstatic love scene in which Elisa's bath overflows, flooding the entire bathroom and leaking into the cinema below, recalled real events. 'I didn't screw a creature,'[19] del Toro hastily pointed out, but as a boy his parents only had a shower, and he longed to swim in a bathtub. So he stuffed towels around the bottom of the shower and blocked the plug. Only when the water reached his chest did he realize that the door opened inwards. He was trapped like Houdini! Forcing it open, the deluge swamped the bathroom floor. 'My father was not happy with the results,'[20] he admitted.

Giles's apartment next door, with its hoarder's clutter and architect's table, carries an echo of Bleak House and Hitchcock's *Vertigo*. Del Toro described his method of decoration as the equivalent of Pop Art, blowing up the everyday into the surreal. Here he highlights the set with a warm, amber, life-giving glow as if it were perpetually sunset or dawn. It is also as liberally strewn with cats as Hellboy's abode.

The laboratory at the Occam Aerospace Research Center is the sum of all the mortuaries, factory floors, workshops, and loci of experimentation in del Toro's multiverse, drawing their inspiration from the original seat of creation in James Whale's *Frankenstein*. It is here, at the centre of a labyrinth, that the river god, as the Amazonian locals had thought of him, is imprisoned, in a cruel variant on Abe's tank in *Hellboy*.

The set was designed around the character. The monumental piping and metal housing evoked the idea of a temple. The adjoining pool, like a lagoon in which the amphibian can surface, is another directorial hallmark. Think back to the cistern in *The Devil's Backbone* where Santi met his fate, or the vat of blood at the centre of Damaskinos's lair in *Blade II*.

Even among del Toro's extensive menagerie, *The Shape of Water* would live or die on its singular creature design. It was asking a lot of viewers to root romantically for a merman. As beautiful as he found him, the original Gill-man was only a starting

Above left: The invisibles – ignored janitors Elisa (Sally Hawkins) and co-worker cum ally Zelda (Octavia Spencer) – will scheme to free the exotic captive.

Above: In contrast to the murky atmosphere of the base, the apartment of Elisa's neighbour Giles (Richard Jenkins) is bathed in warm, golden light.

point. 'I need you to give it a soul,'[21] he told sculptor Mike Hill (who had worked on *The Wolfman* and *Men in Black 3*). It was a fine balance. We needed to perceive both the alien and the human.

The director's notebooks were already crammed with annotated sketches and a working philosophy for capturing life in latex. 'The first thing you have to resolve is the silhouette,' he explained. 'Once the silhouette captures the gait and personality of the character, then you define the colour. Then you define the details.'[22] This is where so many movies go wrong. They start with the details: give me five wings, huge tentacles and teeth! 'They start accumulating,'[23] he said, firmly shaking his head. A great creature is never achieved by accumulation, but coming at each element very carefully.

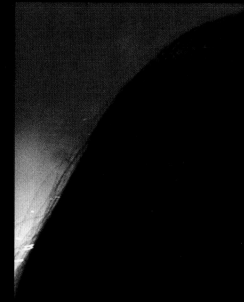

Top: At the heart of the base lies the lab where the amphibious man is held captive, which Guillermo del Toro designed in honour of *Frankenstein's* workshop.

Above: The mute Elisa communicates with her strange paramour via American Sign Language. Sally Hawkins needed to learn it well enough to use in her performance.

Right: One of del Toro's intriguing challenges was that his monster should also be a desirable leading man – which meant that he needed kissable lips!

Encompassing three years of research and development, the amphibian man (the exact species left deliberately ambiguous) marked the longest individual design process in the del Toro pantheon. Moving from paper to clay to digital sculpting, the myriad prototypes were like drafts of a screenplay. Alongside Hill, an entire team filled the Studio in Bleak House, with del Toro insisting he be rooted in real biology. *Hellboy's* Abe lived in a comic-book world, he told them, whereas this amphibian dwelt in ours. Japanese engravings inspired the base colour scheme: nicotine ivory and oyster green. They talked about striations and blood flow, conceiving of a way to make his bioluminescent glow register on film.

Hill gave him the large eyes, high cheekbones and firm square jaw of a matinée idol, and then voluptuous lips with which to kiss the leading lady. A great ass was vital, and every female in del Toro's household was consulted.

In a telling example of how the director conceives of a language of storytelling, he 'knew'[24] he would introduce the creature emerging from the water, revealing only the top half of his head with the camera at surface level. But it was only when he blinked horizontally that you would 'know he is a living thing.'[25] Such micro-expressions utilized a CG technology that had first been developed for *Blade II* – a way of adding nuance to a physical suit, getting the best from both worlds.

The Mexican maestro's tenth film was the apex of his spidery dance with the wonderful Jones. Finally, he was the leading man. Del Toro had first told him about this haunting creature while they were making *Crimson Peak* in 2014. He's the 'Cary Grant of amphibian men,' he declared without irony, making it clear this was to be a performance. 'You have to connect

with her heart,'[26] he told him: Jones needed to consider the creature's needs, his wants, his soul. What was going on *within* him?

'It is only through art that you're able to glimpse otherness,'[27] del Toro wrote in one of his notebooks. Everything in his notes and designs, and across his films, reaches toward the goal of making the strange familiar and meaningful.

'Even as a kid, I knew that monsters were far more gentle and far more desirable than the monsters living inside "nice people,"' he explained. 'I think being a monster, and accepting that you are a monster, gives you the leeway to not behave like one.'[28]

The amphibian, his version of the legendary Gill-man, is charming, powerful, and, indeed, desirable. Del Toro spoke of the statuesque bearing of a toreador.

'It's a spiritual thing,'[29] said Shannon, awe-struck by the grace and otherworldliness Jones could invest into this being. He is deliberately

Christ-like, a god chained by men, with the power to bring back the dead.

As was standard practice, del Toro had written detailed biographies for the main characters. Elisa's chatterbox work friend Zelda (the excellent Spencer), who loved to listen to Dr. King on the radio, had segued from an unhappy childhood into an unhappy marriage. The more misanthropic Giles (Richard Jenkins) is an advertising artist kept on the payroll by an ex, his style long out of fashion. He also serves as the film's narrator. 'I wanted him to be the guy who knew Elisa the best,'[30] said del Toro. Shannon's Strickland, on a rising historical curve from Jacinto in *The Devil's Backbone* and Vidal in *Pan's Labyrinth*, is the film's tragic monster with a human face. Shannon is a nuanced actor who has found depths in heavies as wild as General Zod in *Man of Steel*, and del Toro wanted that mix of brute force and pathos. He's a government man, fixed in his devotion to *his* America, but also another man carrying the scars left by a bad father.

Opposite: A spy movie on the sly – Colonel Strickland (Michael Shannon) confers with chief scientist Hoffstetler (Michael Stuhlbarg), who is not all he seems to be.

Right: Drenched soul – a deranged Strickland is on the hunt for his missing experiment. As with all Guillermo del Toro's villains, there is an element of tragedy to the character.

Below: Despite being set in 1962, *The Shape of Water* was written as a warning to the growing divisions of contemporary times.

Aside from *Mimic*, *The Shape of Water* is del Toro's first film in any meaningful way to be set in his adopted nation, and gets to grips with a particular strain of American paranoia. In 1962, with the Cold War well into its groove, the air was thick with the fear of Reds lurking under beds. Science fiction as a genre had become implanted with metaphors for atomic peril and invasion, where monsters stood for commies, ready to transform ordinary folk into Pod People. Del Toro tips such B-movie convention on its head. Michael Stuhlbarg's sympathetic Dr. Hoffstetler will prove to be the communist sleeper working to stop the Americans weaponizing what is referred to as a 'CIA asset.'[31] In his own way, Hoffstetler is another outsider trapped within this concrete underworld.

There was no need to write a biography for Elisa. Such was the depth of the conversations between director and performer about the inner life of this character, it was clear the work had been done. Hawkins knew Elisa better than anyone. Del Toro had written the

part with the bird-like British actress in mind, drawn to her more talkative yet similarly off-centre roles in *Happy-Go-Lucky* and *Fingersmith*. Hawkins had an inner radiance that made her ethereal, even slightly inexplicable, but not as some naïf. She was womanly.

When her agent mentioned that del Toro was writing a movie for her, Hawkins wouldn't let herself believe it was going to happen. But with uncanny synchronicity, at that very time, she was writing a short film about a woman who didn't know she was a fish. Something like destiny was at work. Director and star began an email correspondence, with del Toro pushing for her input into the script's gradual evolution.

If Strickland hearkened back to the fascistic scoundrels of del Toro's past, Elisa was the grown version of Aurora in *Cronos* (as well as Ofelia from *Pan's Labyrinth*). Hawkins had to become fluent in American Sign Language, enough to express the stirrings of an almost existential level of desire without words. Del Toro presented her with a box filled with the complete

works of Laurel and Hardy, Buster Keaton, Harold Lloyd, and Charlie Chaplin. He wanted that tradition of silent acting – the thrill of body language from the dawn of movies. Most days she forgot she was even playing a mute. Onscreen, her eyes blaze with feeling and meaning. An inner life spills out of her to define the film. While on the surface, scars mark her neck: the mysterious injuries that led to her silence and correspond to gills.

'Love has no shape,'[32] preached del Toro. Like water, it is the most malleable substance in the universe, but under pressure it becomes incredibly powerful. The final shot, maybe the happiest of all his endings, sees the couple embracing in the deep, one red shoe drifting away unheeded.

This was the first movie where he had 'exhaled'[33] afterwards, declared del Toro. All his previous films came with a sense of loss. As if something had gotten away. *The Shape of Water* was complete.

The Mexican Mogul

Directing alone was never going to suffice for the imagination of Guillermo del Toro. He has fingers in many distinctively flavoured pies

AS NOVELIST

The Strain Trilogy (2009-2011)
Co-written with Chuck Hogan, del Toro's first novel, *The Strain* (2009) mixes elements of *Mimic* and *Blade II* as disease control experts race to stall the outbreak of a vampiric virus. A trilogy has since been completed with *The Fall* (2010) and The *Night Eternal* (2011).

Trollhunters (2015)
A teen-orientated novel, co-written with Daniel Kraus, concerning a tribe of child-stealing trolls who lurk beneath the unassuming Californian town of Arcadia Falls.

The Shape of Water (2018) and Pan's Labyrinth: The Labyrinth of the Faun (2019)
Rather than workaday novelizations, del Toro has co-written a pair of literary renditions of his most treasured films, with the assistance of (respectively) Kraus and Cornelia Funke.

The Hollow Ones (2020)
A new series with Hogan, which follows a young FBI agent confronted with ghostly beings able to take possession of humans.

AS TELEVISION PRODUCER

The Strain (2014-2017)
As well as expanding into a series of comic books, del Toro was executive producer on a television adaptation of his forensic-styled vampire novels, starring Corey Stoll and David Bradley. The show ran for four seasons.

Trollhunters: Tales of Arcadia (2016-2018)
Del Toro produced an adaptation of his own novel, *Trollhunters*, as a CG-animated series on Netflix. Such was its success that the show has since expanded into two spin-offs: *3Below* (2018-9) and *Wizards* (2020), involving extra-terrestrial siblings exiled to Earth and twelfth-century Camelot.

AS MOVIE PRODUCER

The Orphanage (2007)
J.A. Bayona's well-regarded tribute to seventies Spanish cinema, following various disappearances and supernatural clues at a haunted orphanage.

Don't Be Afraid of the Dark (2010)
A remake of a 1973 TV-movie, this formulaic slice of Lovecraftian nastiness finds the goblin-like horribles lurking in the basement of a rundown mansion preying on new owners Guy Pearce and Katie Holmes.

Mama (2013)
The provocative horror that launched the career of Andy Muschietti (*It: Chapters One & Two*), in which two wildling sisters sent to live with their uncle (Nikolaj Coster-Waldau) have brought a strange, maternal force with them.

The Book of Life (2014)
This CGI-animated Mexican fable, directed by countryman Jorge R. Gutiérrez, works as grand homage to its producer's penchant for Latin folklore; lovely, tactile detail, and Ron Perlman's baritone (he supplies a voice).

Pacific Rim: Uprising (2018)
This lifeless sequel to the giant robot epic serves as proof that even in his more Hollywood moments del Toro's signature is impossible to copy.

Scary Stories to Tell in the Dark (2019)
Based on Alvin Schwartz's hugely popular novels, various del Toro-like motifs – unsuspecting teens, a supernatural book, a haunted mansion – are given a spirited run-through. At one stage, del Toro thought of directing, before handing control to Norwegian genre-specialist André Øvredal.

AS PURVEYOR OF THE FINEST TEQUILA

Patrón x Guillermo del Toro
Aged for five years and served in a handcrafted bottle, this limited-edition del Toro tequila was made in partnership with Patrón, one of the oldest Mexican distilleries, and has been praised for its sultry caramel character, lively citrus aromas, and supremely dark undercurrents.

THE WEAVER OF DREAMS

Nightmare Alley (2021) & Pinocchio (2021)

How that lonely Mexican boy now stands tall as a major director, with two films due in a single year. One is a starry film noir with mystical leanings, based on a forgotten novel. The other reinvents a classic in lavish stop-motion

It is 2021, and as the writing of this book draws to a close, Guillermo del Toro is an artist in full bloom. In the afterglow of his victory at the Oscars, he had dared to take a year off from filmmaking. But as with most things in his life, joy was often tempered with grief. Shortly after that glorious night, his father passed away. Everything was suddenly put into perspective. How short our time was – and how poignant are our relationships. For many different reasons, deep down he had made every one of his films for his father. That was never going to change.

So he doubled down on his work, quite literally, with two new films due for release before the year's end. An exercise in contrasts, both will break significant new ground, evolving what we understand as del-Toro-esque. Yet each will still bear the director's reassuringly eccentric stamp.

The first finds its origin in a village on the outskirts of Valencia, where the writer William Lindsay Gresham is awaiting repatriation. It is 1938, and all is lost. A restless, often tormented soul, he had signed up as an international volunteer in the futile hope of defending the Republic amid the agonies of the Spanish Civil War.

This fact alone, you suspect, would have drawn del Toro toward his strange flame: another broken, quixotic artist unsung by history. But Gresham offered greater enticements. Born in Baltimore and raised in New York, he had experimented with Marxism and psychoanalysis, but was equally intrigued by spiritualism. He searched both the worlds of reason and the occult for answers. As a boy, he had been spellbound by the fortune-tellers and self-styled mystics holding court in the sideshows at Coney Island.

Right: Guillermo del Toro gazes upon the puppet *Pinocchio*. His stop-motion rendition of the classic story has an autobiographical angle – he has spent his entire career bringing puppets to life

As he waited for his ship, he drank. Joining him at his table was Joseph Daniel 'Doc' Halliday, a fellow American who had once laboured as a carnie in the travelling shows that rattled from state to state, offering meagre distraction from the miseries of the Depression. It was Halliday who first told Gresham about the geek. He explained that a geek was about the lowest form of entertainment. This was a drunk so desperate that he would sit in a cage and bite the heads from chickens and snakes on the promise of hooch. The geek was about as low as a man could fall.

Gresham couldn't shake that image – the emaciated fool with his bloody grin. He knew the pull of the bottle and the destitution that followed, and perhaps the idea of this fallen man hit close to home. 'Finally, to get rid of it,' he said, 'I had to write it out.'[1] On his return from Spain, he began the novel for which he is best known and would form the basis of del Toro's next film.

Published in 1946 to brief acclaim, and set against the backdrop of the Depression, *Nightmare Alley* tells the story of Stanton Carlisle (Bradley Cooper), a conman with a silken tongue, who works his way up from fronting for a carnival medium to running intricate scams as a spiritualist-preacher, before finding his most daring mark in a wealthy industrialist named Ezra Grindle (Richard Jenkins). Meanwhile, he will fall into an uncertain partnership with the enchanting psychiatrist and potential femme fatale Lilith Ritter (Cate Blanchett).

A cypher for the long-suffering author, Stanton is the most morally ambiguous of all del Toro's characters. He recalls a childhood of bitter fathers and unfaithful mothers. The sins of the parents are passed onto the lonely son, who neglects his sweet wife Molly (Rooney Mara) as he is drawn into the web spun by Lilith, haunted all the while by his first glimpse of a geek in the travelling show. This is unsparing film noir territory.

A previous, black-and-white, straight noir adaptation, from 1947, starred Tyrone Power, desperate to get out of the swashbuckling game. But studio head Darryl F. Zanuck had been so horrified by the downbeat ending that he had limited its release, leaving it to languish on the midnight circuit.

There is no doubting del Toro's love for the hothouse genres. By 2020, he had laid claim to the worlds of horror, superhero, fairy-tale, and science fiction, often standing astride their borders like one of the great Jaegers from *Pacific Rim*. 'I don't think it's in my DNA,'[2] he replied when asked if he would ever make a straight drama. He had made genre respectable. Horror, he once said, was not a stepping stone but a cathedral.

Yet he ached to try film noir.

Noir is harder to place. It is as much a style as a genre. In the main, it represents a run of postwar thrillers marked by their taut psychology, claustrophobia, highly stylized settings, and a nihilistic take on human nature.

Right: A poster for Edmund Goulding's 1947 film adaptation of William Lindsay Gresham's novel. The studio removed its scenes of gruesome attacks on chickens before release.

Right: *Nightmare Alley* co-writer Kim Morgan at the Oscars with del Toro in 2017. The former film critic had also worked on Canadian surrealist Guy Maddin's horror movie *The Forbidden Room* (2015).

In the shadowy, urban realms of noir, villain and heroes come clothed alike.

'I'm really quite taken by the period between the late thirties and the mid forties, where the world is changed by World War Two,' he stated in 2015, directing his thoughts toward the heartland of noir. 'I would love to do a historic drama, but I need to do it around an anecdote that is at the very least outlandish enough to attract my imagination. I knock on wood, and I hope it happens one day.'[3]

It turned out he already had the perfectly outlandish noir in his hands. Ron Perlman had given him a copy of *Nightmare Alley* in 1992, when they were making *Cronos*. Del Toro was struck by its savage tone and divination of where the American Dream was headed. 'In the book there was sort of a disillusionment with capitalism, and a disillusionment with quote-unquote civilization of the urban environment,' he said. 'I thought it was very sexually

charged, and really poignant about America, with a brilliant intuitive connection between carnival mentalism and the birth of psychology in America.'[4]

In 2017, he set to work on a new adaptation with co-writer Kim Morgan (*The Forbidden Room*). 'Now is the first chance I have to do a real "underbelly of society" type of movie,'[5] he reported eagerly.

Produced by Searchlight Pictures, it was another relatively conservative production. Nevertheless, del Toro attracted a sensational cast. In a true measure of the respect in which he was now held, when he missed out on Leonardo DiCaprio as his fast-talking lead due to scheduling issues then Cooper stepped into the breach. Around him, del Toro assembled old friends and lucky charms like Ron Perlman and Jenkins in significant parts. Plus, interesting new colours for the canvas

in Blanchett, Mara, Toni Collette, Willem Dafoe, and David Strathairn.

While noir flirts with horror, offering elusive, nightmarish, violent, and surreal stories, according to del Toro, there are 'no supernatural elements.'[6] This is a relative distinction. *Nightmare Alley* is by no means a straight drama. Connective tissue to his other work is readily apparent. This is still very much a Guillermo del Toro movie.

For one thing, there is a striking parallel between the elaborate tricks executed by Stanton to fool his congregants and filmmaking itself, which essentially uses a sophisticated sleight-of-hand to dupe an audience into belief. At high school, del Toro was famed for his elaborate pranks. He is still doing much the same thing. So there is a touch of autobiography to this (con) artist living by his wits.

Gresham killed himself in 1962, the demons finally gaining sway, his body

discovered in a rundown New York hotel room. Like H.P. Lovecraft, he went uncelebrated in his day, but a cult has sprung up around his acerbic fiction. He is another of the shadowy, tragic, misunderstood figures from the literary fringes with whom del Toro so often finds a kinship. Curiously, Gresham's first wife was the poet Joy Davidman, who would later marry Narnia creator C.S. Lewis, before dying young – a tragedy depicted in the Richard Attenborough film *Shadowlands*.

And there is something mystical at loose in the book. During the writing, Gresham had drifted into an obsession with the Tarot – the deck of pictorial cards that in the right hands can, supposedly, foretell the future.

As well as being used in the story by the medium Zeena, the novel is structured around the twenty-two trump cards, or Major Arcana: each chapter falling under the heading, and persuasion, of pictograms such as The Fool, The Hanged Man, and The Lovers. This lends the story a subtext. Maybe there is a greater power at work. In other words, this

is a film noir tuned into the mystical. From the humble farmers duped by the carnies, to Stanton's enraptured followers, to the well-heeled mark, everyone hungers for meaning from the universe. Whether psychological or spiritual, Stanton has a destiny he cannot escape. Life itself is a confidence trick.

'An unexpected turn is always one card away,' said del Toro, 'and, in that, the Tarot is like life itself.'[7] As he could have informed Gresham, Freud had made it clear in a study 'of the so-called occult facts'[8] that the Tarot could no longer be dismissed.

This focus on the symbolic cards struck another chime with the director's childhood. 'My mother read the Tarot to anyone that would ask her – regardless of the time or setting,' recalled del Toro. 'She always carried a deck of cards, nestled in a velvet pouch inside her handbag, and treated it with great care and respect. The edges of the cards were worn and stained from the frequency and familiarity of their handling.'[9]

His mother also taught him the I Ching, palmistry, and how to read

Above left: Bradley Cooper was ideal casting for charismatic conman Stanton Carlisle. Shoots in 2020 were disrupted by the pandemic, and Cooper completed Paul Thomas Anderson's *Soggy Bottom* in the middle of *Nightmare Alley*.

Above right: Having previously starred opposite one another in Todd Haynes' *Carol*, Cate Blanchett and Rooney Mara feature as Lilith Ritter and Molly Cahill – the two women who would shape Stanton's destiny.

Opposite: Starring real circus performers, Tod Browning's controversial 1932 classic *Freaks* has long fascinated del Toro, and is the direct inspiration for his depiction of the denizens of a travelling carnival.

tea leaves. Such dark arts were far more alluring to his young imagination than the worldly lessons of a pragmatic father or the dogma of a staunchly Catholic grandmother.

The Tarot offered a secret, symbolic code that del Toro has applied to his films so that they might be read the same way. 'Symbols tap to the cosmic root of our being,' he claimed. '… I started using the Tarot not only as a storytelling device, but to hone my storytelling intuition.'[10] Indeed, a *Tarot del Toro* was published in 2020, illustrated with hand-painted linocuts based on his films by the Spanish artist Tomás Hijo (celebrated for his depictions of Lovecraft and Tolkien). Del Toro himself is portrayed as The Magician, the weaver of dreams.

Furthermore, while it had no monsters per se, the novel presented an array of freakshow regulars for del Toro to bring to vivid and sympathetic life. These include a strongman, a 'Half-man Acrobat'[11] with withered legs who walks on his hands, and a character going by the name Fee Fee the Birdgirl.

Tod Browning's *Freaks* is a key inspiration. This haunting 1932 horror cast genuinely deformed sideshow performers to play a circus troupe that enacts a terrible revenge on a duplicitous trapeze artist. Released to outrage and box office ruin, another very particular cult has since swelled around this unclassifiable marvel. Naturally, del Toro is a fully paid-up member.

Using his Twitter account to right wrongs, championing forgotten films, he described *Freaks* as a singularity. 'There has never been and will never be a film like this again,'[12] he declared.

All of which makes *Nightmare Alley* a fascinating contradiction: a break with the norm, a character-driven drama, a layered con-movie, a portrait of America, a bleak existential trip, and another exercise in juggling genres like knives.

Shooting kicked off in January 2020, with Toronto playing variously New York and the stops on the carnival trail. However, world events that carried an ominous echo of a del Toro storyline (especially that of *The Strain*) would bring proceedings to a dramatic halt in March 2020, with not quite half the film shot. The COVID-19 pandemic closed down all production, sending Hollywood scheduling into disarray.

'We were literally in the middle of a great scene,' reported del Toro. 'We went to lunch and talked to the studio and when we came back we said, "Everybody leave your tools and leave now."'[13]

Even when they were given the go-ahead to restart, del Toro had to wait for Cooper to finish shooting another film (with director Paul Thomas Anderson), which had begun shortly before. But he had not been idle. Rather than stew in his creative juices, he was able to give his full attention to *Pinocchio*.

Concurrent to the live-action complexities of *Nightmare Alley*, del Toro was attempting a new medium entirely. With his adoration of Ray Harryhausen, and the surrealist worlds of Czech animator Jan Švankmajer, del Toro longed to make a stop-motion film. He had already used the technique to depict the creation of mechanical soldiers in the prologue to *Hellboy II: The Golden Army*, as well as unsuccessfully pitching a stop-motion adaptation of Roald Dahl's *The Witches*. Robert Zemeckis would finally bring del Toro's screenplay for this to the screen in a scurry of cartoonish CGI and live action in 2020.

'I've been an animator all my life,' insisted del Toro. 'The first movies I made were stop-motion with my Super 8 camera. I love the medium.'[14]

Pinocchio had passed through the almost inevitable long gestation. He began working on the screenplay with longtime collaborator and mentor Matthew Robbins. Part of the revolutionary Movie Brat scene in the seventies, Robbins had worked with Spielberg, Lucas, and Coppola. He had also directed the piquant fantasy *Dragonslayer*, which del Toro adored. Invited to Guadalajara to help run a series of workshops with emerging writers, Robbins recalled being assigned to this 'oddball twenty-nine-year-old character,'[15] and they have never stopped talking.

Starting with *Mimic*, they have collaborated on ten screenplays, including *Pinocchio*, which Robbins was working on while del Toro was still in New Zealand with *The Hobbit*. 'It was,' by Robbins's estimation, 'about as far as you can get from the Disney-fied version.'[16]

Del Toro sees it as more of a reorientation of the traditionally animated 1940 movie. He won't have a word said against Walt Disney. 'I believe the man changed the way we tell stories,'[17] he decreed, and those animated classics occupy their own little corner of his imagination. The Disney version of *Pinocchio* was a coming-of-age journey through a phantasmagorical world. The scenes of kids being turned into donkeys were highly disturbing. It delivered what del Toro deemed the necessary "darkness"[18] of a fairy-tale.

Nevertheless, he was working with a greater dedication to the more surreal style of the original 1883 novel by Carlo Collodi. 'Pinocchio has strange moments of lucid dreaming bordering on hallucinations … The many mishaps Pinocchio goes through include several near-death close calls, a lot more harrowing moments.'[19] And with a typical emphasis on what he

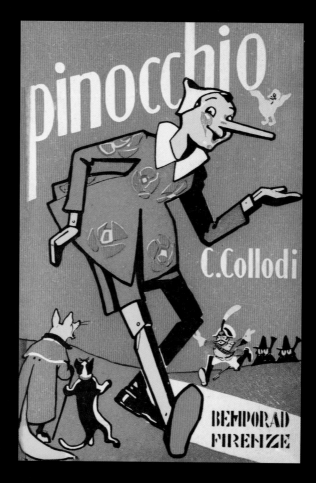

saw as the political aspect in Collodi's work. The film's setting will be proto-fascist 1930s Italy. As Robbins saw it, the subtext of the story was 'the idea of freedom that goes too far into chaos.'[20]

This is to be a celebration of the creative anarchy that comes with breaking the rules: a theme that goes back to the rebellious boys of *The Devil's Backbone*, *Hellboy*, and Ofelia's self-determination in *Pan's Labyrinth*. Disobedience, preached del Toro, cuts both ways.

So there is a tincture of self-portrait thrown in for good measure. Growing up, he had felt a kinship with Pinocchio. 'I was very interested in whether he can be himself and be loved. Does he have to turn into a real boy to be loved?'[21]

Del Toro wanted to celebrate imperfections.

Naturally, this is where *Frankenstein* rears his ugly-beautiful head – the concept of a created soul. 'He's a creature that's created through unnatural means by a father that he distances himself from and has to learn the ways of the world by failing and ache and pain and loneliness,'[22] said del Toro, delighting in how different this was from the way people tend to perceive *Pinocchio*. His whole approach was autobiographical.

Think about it. Within the story, Geppetto is a man who makes a doll that comes to life. Pinocchio is *actually* a puppet, not a puppet playing a living thing. This is the fictional variant on del Toro's life's work – the director's process writ large. And there is something doubly surreal about portraying a 'living' puppet within a stop-motion world where we are *already* asked to see puppets as living things.

All of which makes for exactly the kind of ironies and textures to ward away studio investment. But del Toro stuck to his guns. These were characters with extreme personalities. He wanted that handmade feel, the warp and weft of real material, even if it cost $35 million.

'I've gone through every studio in Hollywood,' he insisted, 'and they all said no.'[23] It was Netflix that came to his rescue. The streaming giant was proving adventurous in its choices, having recently made *The Ballad of Buster Scruggs* with the Coen brothers and *Roma* with his old friend Alfonso Cuarón. Both films that del Toro has sung to the rafters. Moreover, he had already partnered with Netflix on the successful computer animated series *Trollhunters* (a *Hellboy*-like tale of a monster-fighting suburban boy). Even if he had to forego a cinema release, he would be able to make the film as he chose, drawing on Japanese Bunraku puppet theatre, where the puppets have highly expressive faces as white as ghosts. And adding a musical element: since Robbins's involvement, Patrick McHale has rewritten the screenplay to include songs, with del Toro and rapper Katz providing the lyrics, and a score by Alexandre Desplat.

Left: Geppetto introduces Pinocchio to the startled cat in one of Attilio Mussino's famous 1911 illustrations. Del Toro draws on the character's many previous guises, but invests it with his distinctive house style.

Production began on 31 January 2020 out of ShadowMachine Studios in Portland, Oregon, and – under tightly controlled studio conditions – continued uninterrupted through the pandemic. Stop-motion is an arduous process. Barely seconds of footage are achieved each day. So del Toro brought in co-director Mark Gustafson to bear the time-consuming load. Gustafson was well versed in channelling the whims of an auteur, having worked as an animation director on Wes Anderson's *Fantastic Mr. Fox*.

Mackinnon and Saunders Ltd., purveyors of miniature characters with a gothic hue to such films as *Corpse Bride*, *Coraline*, and *The Boxtrolls*, built the puppets. Their distinctive designs were based on the work of children's author and illustrator Gris Grimly (who was due to direct an early iteration of the project), celebrated for his distinctive take on the tales of Edgar Allan Poe, *The Legend of Sleepy Hollow*, and a 2002 edition of Collodi's *The Adventures of Pinocchio*. Grimly is another collaborator tuned to the

same frequencies as the director: his macabre, comic-book flourishes recall Charles Addams, Edward Gorey, Tim Burton, and the nightmarish visions of German Expressionism.

With spindle-like limbs and a spherical head, Pinocchio (newcomer Gregory Mann) recalls the chittering fairies from *Pan's Labyrinth* and *Hellboy II: The Golden Army*. The Cricket ('Jiminy' being a Disney affectation) is fully that – a talking insect voiced by Ewan McGregor. And with his large Coke-bottle glasses and wispy moustache, Geppetto (David Bradley) resembles a raggedy version of Professor Broom from *Hellboy*.

The voice cast was filled out with another impressive mix of familiar del Toro players and those for whom you sense it was only a matter of time, including Cate Blanchett, Tilda Swinton, Tim Blake Nelson, Christoph Waltz, John Turturro, and that comforting thunderstorm Ron Perlman.

Nightmare Alley finally wrapped on 14 December 2020, and is slated

Below left: Christoph Waltz gives voice to both the Fox and Cat, a pair of tricksters who, in the Collodi original, waylay poor Pinocchio and attempt to murder him.

Below centre: Tilda Swinton lends her velvety tonsils to the Fairy with Turquoise Hair – a thousand-year-old fairy who will eventually be Pinocchio's saviour.

Below right: David Bradley gives his gravelly tones to Mister Geppetto, the impoverished woodcarver who creates Pinocchio from a block of pinewood.

for release on 3 December 2021, confidently at the heart of awards season. *Pinocchio* is also slated for release in 2021 to complete the most productive year in del Toro's remarkable career.

At 56, this brilliant filmmaker, the geek who has inherited the world, takes delight in the fact he is impossible to summarize. 'I don't belong in any safe film category: too weird for full-on summer fare, too in love with pop culture for the art house world, and too esoteric for hardcore fandom. The fact is, every premise I am attracted to has an inherent risk of failure. I often find myself wondering why I cannot choose an easier path.'[24]

Yet it is because he has followed his own instincts through strange labyrinths that he has emerged as one of the most singular and wonderful voices in modern cinema. You could say he is the least Hollywood of Hollywood directors, or the most Mexican. A member of that tight band of filmmakers who will always be sought out as much for what they make as how they make it. With each film our expectations are always high for this mad creation: part Grimm, part Lovecraft, part Harryhausen, part Buñuel, part Marx brother, part Corman, part Spielberg, and always himself.

Reading the cards for what the future may hold, there are numerous directions he could turn in, scripts and treatments and notebooks brimming with ideas (and monsters) on the polished shelves of Bleak House. But as he develops a project, or receives a lucrative offer, or waits for the gods to instruct him, he keeps one thing in mind.

'I always ask myself, "Would this movie exist if I didn't make it?" And if the answer is yes, I don't do it.'[25]

Above: Del Toro becomes the 2,669th star on Hollywood Boulevard in 2019. As he accepted the honour, he clutched a tricolor Mexican flag and pressed it to his lips.

SOURCES

Introduction

1. *The Merriam-Webster Dictionary*, Turtleback Books, 2016
2. *Guillermo del Toro – Cabinet of Curiosities: My Notebooks, Collections, and Other Obsessions*, Guillermo del Toro and Marc Scott Zicree, Titan Books, 2013
3. *10 Questions for Guillermo del Toro*, Gilbert Cruz, *Time*, 5 September 2011
4. *Guillermo del Toro's Pan's Labyrinth*, Nick Nunziata, Mark Cotta Vaz, and Guillermo del Toro, Titan Books, 2016

Once Upon a Time in Mexico

1. *Pan's Labyrinth Blu-ray Edition*, The Criterion Edition, 18 October 2016
2. *Guillermo del Toro – Guardian Interviews at the BFI*, Mark Kermode, 21 November 2006
3. *Guillermo del Toro's Pan's Labyrinth*, Nick Nunziata, Mark Cotta Vaz, and Guillermo del Toro, Titan Books, 2016
4. Ibid.
5. *Guillermo del Toro on Confronting Childhood Demons and Surviving a Real-life Horror Story*, Stephen Galloway, Hollywood Reporter, 3 November 2017
6. *Guillermo del Toro's Pan's Labyrinth*, Nick Nunziata, Mark Cotta Vaz, and Guillermo del Toro, Titan Books, 2016
7. *Guillermo del Toro – Cronos Interviews*, The Criterion Edition, 7 December 2010
8. *Guillermo del Toro Masterclass*, Lumière Festival, Lyon, France on 13 October 2018
9. *Guillermo del Toro – Guardian Interviews at the BFI*, Mark Kermode, *The Guardian*, 21 November 2006
10. *Guillermo del Toro – Cronos Interviews*, The Criterion Edition, 7 December 2010
11. Ibid.
12. *Pan's Labyrinth – BFI Film Classics*, Mar Diestro-Dópido, Bloomsbury, 2013
13. *Guillermo del Toro Interview – Blade II, Capture Magazine* via YouTube, 2012
14. *Guillermo del Toro's Pan's Labyrinth*, Nick Nunziata, Mark Cotta Vaz, and Guillermo del Toro, Titan Books, 2016
15. Ibid.
16. *Guillermo del Toro – Cabinet of Curiosities: My Notebooks, Collections, and Other Obsessions*, Guillermo del Toro and Marc Scott Zicree, Titan Books, 2013
17. *Guillermo del Toro's The Devil's Backbone*, Matt Zoller Seitz & Simon Abrams, Titan Books, 2017
18. *Guillermo del Toro – Cabinet of Curiosities: My Notebooks, Collections, and Other Obsessions*, Guillermo del Toro and Marc Scott Zicree, Titan Books, 2013
19. *Guillermo del Toro's The Devil's Backbone*, Matt Zoller Seitz & Simon Abrams, Titan Books, 2017
20. *Guillermo del Toro – Cabinet of Curiosities: My Notebooks, Collections, and Other Obsessions*, Guillermo del Toro and Marc Scott Zicree, Titan Books, 2013
21. *Guillermo del Toro's The Devil's Backbone*, Matt Zoller Seitz & Simon Abrams, Titan Books, 2017

22. *Show The Monster*, Daniel Zalewski, *The New Yorker*, 31 January 2011
23. *Guillermo del Toro – Cabinet of Curiosities: My Notebooks, Collections, and Other Obsessions*, Guillermo del Toro and Marc Scott Zicree, Titan Books, 2013
24. Ibid.
25. *The Craft of the Director: Guillermo del Toro, Directors Guild of America* via YouTube, 7 May 2018
26. *Guillermo del Toro – Cabinet of Curiosities: My Notebooks, Collections, and Other Obsessions*, Guillermo del Toro and Marc Scott Zicree, Titan Books, 2013
27. *Guillermo del Toro – Cronos Interviews*, The Criterion Edition, 7 December 2010
28. Ibid.
29. Ibid.
30. Ibid.
31. Ibid.
32. *Guillermo del Toro – Cronos Interviews*, The Criterion Edition, 7 December 2010
33. *Cronos Interview Part 1, Studiocanal* via YouTube, 11 May 2008
34. Ibid.
35. *Guillermo del Toro – Cabinet of Curiosities: My Notebooks, Collections, and Other Obsessions*, Guillermo del Toro and Marc Scott Zicree, Titan Books, 2013
36. Cronos interview via YouTube, 11 May, 2008
37. *Guillermo del Toro's Pan's Labyrinth*, Nick Nunziata, Mark Cotta
38. *Cronos Interview Part 1, Studiocanal* via YouTube, 11 May 2008
39. *Cronos: Alive With Charms Eternal*, Kenneth Turan, *The Los Angeles Times*, 22 April 1994
40. *Guillermo del Toro's Pan's Labyrinth*, Nick Nunziata, Mark Cotta Vaz, and Guillermo del Toro, Titan Books, 2016
41. Ibid.
42. *Guillermo del Toro – Cronos Interviews*, The Criterion Edition, 7 December 2010
43. *Guillermo del Toro's The Devil's Backbone*, Matt Zoller Seitz & Simon Abrams, Titan Books, 2017
44. *Cronos Interview Part 1, Studiocanal* via YouTube, 11 May 2008
45. *Guillermo del Toro – Cabinet of Curiosities: My Notebooks, Collections, and Other Obsessions*, Guillermo del Toro and Marc Scott Zicree, Titan Books, 2013
46. Ibid.
47. *Guillermo del Toro's The Devil's Backbone*, Matt Zoller Seitz & Simon Abrams, Titan Books, 2017
48. *Guillermo del Toro – Cronos Interviews*, The Criterion Edition, 7 December 2010
49. *Guillermo del Toro – Cabinet of Curiosities: My Notebooks, Collections, and Other Obsessions*, Guillermo del Toro and Marc Scott Zicree, Titan Books, 2013
50. *Cronos Interview Part 1, Studiocanal* via YouTube, 11 May 2008
51. *Guillermo del Toro – Cabinet of Curiosities: My Notebooks, Collections, and Other Obsessions*, Guillermo del Toro and Marc Scott Zicree, Titan Books, 2013

52. *Blu-ray Review: Guillermo del Toro's Cronos on the Criterion Collection*, Glenn Heath Jr., Slant, 10 December 2010
53. *Pan's Labyrinth – BFI Film Classics*, Mar Diestro-Dópido, Bloomsbury, 2013
54. *Guillermo del Toro - Interviews: Cronos*, The Criterion Edition, 7 December 2010
55. Ibid.
56. Ibid.
57. *Guillermo del Toro Q&A, deltorofilms.com*, 2003

Tunnel Vision

1. *Guillermo del Toro Interview*, Geoffrey Macnab, *Independent*, 7 February 2018
2. *Down and Dirty Pictures*, Peter Biskind, Simon & Schuster, 2004
3. *Guillermo del Toro – Cabinet of Curiosities: My Notebooks, Collections, and Other Obsessions*, Guillermo del Toro and Marc Scott Zicree, Titan Books, 2013
4. Ibid.
5. *Guillermo del Toro's The Devil's Backbone*, Matt Zoller Seitz & Simon Abrams, Titan Books, 2017
6. *Down and Dirty Pictures*, Peter Biskind, Simon & Schuster, 2004
7. *The Faber Book of Mexican Cinema*, Jason Wood, Faber & Faber, 2006
8. *Guillermo del Toro 'Hated the Experience' of Working With Harvey Weinstein on 'Mimic'*, Zack Sharf, *IndieWire*, 12 October 2017
9. *Guillermo del Toro – Cabinet of Curiosities: My Notebooks, Collections, and Other Obsessions*, Guillermo del Toro and Marc Scott Zicree, Titan Books, 2013
10. Ibid.
11. *Guillermo del Toro – Guardian Interviews at the BFI*, Mark Kermode, *The Guardian*, 21 November 2006
12. *Guillermo del Toro's The Devil's Backbone*, Matt Zoller Seitz & Simon Abrams, Titan Books, 2017
13. *Down and Dirty Pictures*, Peter Biskind, Simon & Schuster, 2004
14. *Guillermo del Toro's The Devil's Backbone*, Matt Zoller Seitz & Simon Abrams, Titan Books, 2017
15. *Guillermo del Toro – Guardian Interviews at the BFI*, Mark Kermode, *The Guardian*, 21 November 2006
16. *Mimic review*, Owen Gleiberman, *Entertainment Weekly*, 7 September 2011
17. *Guillermo del Toro – Cronos Interviews*, The Criterion Edition, 7 December 2010
18. *Mimic review*, Roger Ebert, *Chicago Sun-Times*, 22 August 1997
19. *Guillermo del Toro interview* Nicholas Braccia, *Feo Armante's Horrorthriller.com*, undated
20. *Mimic Director's Cut Blu-ray review*, Chris Holt, *Starburst*, 11 May 2011
21. *Guillermo del Toro and Mira Sorvino interview*, Charlie Rose, *charlierose.com*, 11 August 1997
22. *Guillermo del Toro – Cabinet of Curiosities: My Notebooks, Collections, and Other Obsessions*, Guillermo del Toro and Marc Scott Zicree, Titan Books, 2013

23. Ibid.
24. Ibid.
25. *Guillermo del Toro's Pan's Labyrinth*, Nick Nunziata, Mark Cotta Vaz, and Guillermo del Toro, Titan Books, 2016
26. *Guillermo del Toro Interview*, Geoffrey Macnab, *Independent*, 7 February 2018

Unfinished Business

1. *Empire Meets Guillermo del Toro*, Chris Hewitt, *Empire*, 8 October 2015
2. *Guillermo del Toro's The Devil's Backbone*, Matt Zoller Seitz & Simon Abrams, Titan Books, 2017
3. *Guillermo del Toro – Cabinet of Curiosities: My Notebooks, Collections, and Other Obsessions*, Guillermo del Toro and Marc Scott Zicree, Titan Books, 2013
4. *Interview: No Mimic; Guillermo del Toro Declares His Independence with Devil's Backbone*, Anthony Kaufman, *IndieWire*, 27 November 2001
5. *Guillermo del Toro's The Devil's Backbone*, Matt Zoller Seitz & Simon Abrams, Titan Books, 2017
6. Ibid.
7. *Guillermo del Toro – Cabinet of Curiosities: My Notebooks, Collections, and Other Obsessions*, Guillermo del Toro and Marc Scott Zicree, Titan Books, 2013
8. *Guillermo del Toro interview – The Devil's Backbone*, Stephen Applebaum, *BBC.com*, archived 28 October 2014
9. *Pan's Labyrinth – Interview with Guillermo del Toro*, Michael Guillen, *Screen Anarchy*, 17 December 2006
10. *Guillermo del Toro's The Devil's Backbone*, Matt Zoller Seitz & Simon Abrams, Titan Books, 2017
11. Ibid.
12. Ibid.
13. *Guillermo del Toro – Cabinet of Curiosities: My Notebooks, Collections, and Other Obsessions*, Guillermo del Toro and Marc Scott Zicree, Titan Books, 2013
14. *The Devil's Backbone Blu-ray*, The Criterion Edition, 30 July 2013
15. *Guillermo del Toro interview*, Stephen Applebaum, *BBC.com*, archived 28 October 2014
16. *Guillermo del Toro's The Devil's Backbone*, Matt Zoller Seitz & Simon Abrams, Titan Books, 2017
17. Ibid.
18. Ibid.
19. Ibid.
20. Ibid.
21. *10 Questions for Guillermo del Toro*, Gilbert Cruz, *Time*, 5 September 2011
22. *Interview: No Mimic; Guillermo del Toro Declares His Independence with Devil's Backbone*, Anthony Kaufman, *IndieWire*, 27 November 2001
23. Ibid.
24. Ibid.
25. *Guillermo del Toro's The Devil's Backbone*, Matt Zoller Seitz & Simon Abrams, Titan Books, 2017
26. Ibid.
27. *Guillermo del Toro – Cabinet of Curiosities: My Notebooks, Collections, and Other Obsessions*, Guillermo del Toro and Marc Scott Zicree, Titan Books, 2013
28. *Guillermo del Toro's The Devil's Backbone*, Matt Zoller Seitz & Simon Abrams, Titan Books, 2017
29. *The Devil's Backbone review*, Kevin Thomas, *The Los Angeles Times*, 14 December 2001

30. *Guillermo del Toro's The Devil's Backbone*, Matt Zoller Seitz & Simon Abrams, Titan Books, 2017

Blood Rush

1. *Guillermo del Toro interview – Blade II*, James Mottram, *BBC.com*, archived 24 September 2014
2. Ibid.
3. *Guillermo del Toro Interviewed – Pan's Labyrinth*, Steve 'Frosty' Weintraub, *Collider*, 3 January 2007
4. *Guillermo del Toro – Guardian Interviews at the BFI*, Mark Kermode, *The Guardian*, 21 November 2006
5. Ibid.
6. *Guillermo del Toro Interview – Blade II, Capture Magazine* via YouTube, 2012
7. *Show The Monster*, Daniel Zalewski, *The New Yorker*, 31 January 2011
8. *Guillermo del Toro Interviewed – Pan's Labyrinth*, Steve 'Frosty' Weintraub, *Collider*, 3 January 2007
9. Ibid.
10. *Guillermo del Toro Interview – Blade II, Capture Magazine* via YouTube, 2012
11. *Guillermo del Toro Interview, Daily Motion* via YouTube, 5 November 2011
12. *Jim Brown: the Fierce Life of an American Hero*, Mike Freeman, Harper Collins, 2007
13. *Guillermo del Toro interview – Blade II*, James Mottram, *BBC.com*, archived 24 September 2014
14. *Guillermo del Toro Interview – Blade II, Capture Magazine* via YouTube, 2012
15. *Guillermo del Toro – Guardian Interviews at the BFI*, Mark Kermode, *The Guardian*, 21 November 2006
16. Ibid.
17. *Guillermo del Toro's 15 Year Video Game Saga*, Nic Reuben, *The Face*, 4 October 2019
18. Ibid.
19. Ibid.
20. *Blade II Blu-ray*, Entertainment-video, 2007
21. *Guillermo del Toro interview – Blade II*, James Mottram, *BBC.com*, archived 24 September 2014
22. *Guillermo del Toro Interview – Blade II, Capture Magazine* via YouTube, 2012
23. Ibid.
24. Ibid.
25. *Guillermo del Toro – Guardian Interviews at the BFI*, Mark Kermode, 21 November 2006
26. *Guillermo del Toro – Cabinet of Curiosities: My Notebooks, Collections, and Other Obsessions*, Guillermo del Toro and Marc Scott Zicree, Titan Books, 2013
27. *Guillermo del Toro interview – Blade II*, James Mottram, *BBC.com*, archived 24 September 2014
28. *Guillermo del Toro – Cabinet of Curiosities: My Notebooks, Collections, and Other Obsessions*, Guillermo del Toro and Marc Scott Zicree, Titan Books, 2013
29. *Blade II review*, Roger Ebert, *Chicago Sun-Times*, 22 March 2002
30. *Blade II Blu-ray*, Entertainment-video, 2007
31. *Blade II review*, Roger Ebert, *Chicago Sun-Times*, 22 March 2002
32. *Guillermo del Toro's The Devil's Backbone*, Matt Zoller Seitz & Simon Abrams, Titan Books, 2017
33. *Blade II review*, Ed Gonzalez, *Slant*, 10 March 2002
34. *Guillermo del Toro Interview – Blade II, Capture Magazine* via YouTube, 2012

35. *Interview: Guillermo del Toro*, Paul Fischer, *Moviehole*, 2008
36. *Guillermo del Toro – Cabinet of Curiosities: My Notebooks, Collections, and Other Obsessions*, Guillermo del Toro and Marc Scott Zicree, Titan Books, 2013
37. Ibid.
38. *10 Questions for Guillermo del Toro*, Gilbert Cruz, *Time*, 5 September 2011
39. *Guillermo del Toro – Cabinet of Curiosities: My Notebooks, Collections, and Other Obsessions*, Guillermo del Toro and Marc Scott Zicree, Titan Books, 2013
40. Ibid.
41. *Guillermo del Toro – Guardian Interviews at the BFI*, Mark Kermode, *The Guardian*, 21 November 2006

Sidebar: The Three Amigos

1. *Exclusive: Guillermo del Toro on Netflix, Roma, and Why He's Making Pinocchio*, Helen Barlow, *Collider*, 21 December, 2018
2. Ibid.
3. *BFI Screen Talk: Guillermo del Toro*, BFI London Film Festival via YouTube, 6 December 2017
4. *Exclusive: Guillermo del Toro on Netflix, Roma, and Why He's Making Pinocchio*, Helen Barlow, *Collider*, 21 December, 2018

Big Red

1. *Pan's Labyrinth: A Story that Needed Guillermo del Toro*, unattributed, *Awardsdaily.com*, 2006
2. *Guillermo del Toro – Cabinet of Curiosities: My Notebooks, Collections, and Other Obsessions*, Guillermo del Toro and Marc Scott Zicree, Titan Books, 2013
3. Ibid.
4. *Guillermo del Toro: The Monster Man*, Jonathan Romney, *Independent*, 19 November 2006
5. *Guillermo del Toro's Pan's Labyrinth*, Nick Nunziata, Mark Cotta Vaz, and Guillermo del Toro, Titan Books, 2016
6. *Hellboy presentation*, Comic-Con 2002
7. *Guillermo del Toro Q&A*, deltorofilms.com, 2003
8. *How I Made Hellboy in My Image*, Guillermo del Toro, *The Guardian*, 27 July 2008
9. *Hellboy presentation*, Comic-Con 2002
10. *A Conversation with Guillermo del Toro*, Jeff Otto, *IGN*, 31 May 2012
11. *Guillermo del Toro – Cabinet of Curiosities: My Notebooks, Collections, and Other Obsessions*, Guillermo del Toro and Marc big Scott Zicree, Titan Books, 2013
12. *Hellboy presentation*, Comic-Con 2002
13. Ibid.
14. Ibid.
15. *Guillermo del Toro: What Allowed Hellboy Films to Be Made No Longer Exists*, Zack Sharf, 27 April 2020
16. Ibid.
17. *Guillermo del Toro Q&A*, deltorofilms.com, 2003
18. *Hellboy presentation*, Comic-Con 2002
19. *Guillermo del Toro – Cabinet of Curiosities: My Notebooks, Collections, and Other Obsessions*, Guillermo del Toro and Marc Scott Zicree, Titan Books, 2013
20. *Hellboy Blu-ray 4K*, Sony Pictures, 14 October 2019

21. *Guillermo del Toro's The Devil's Backbone*, Matt Zoller Seitz & Simon Abrams, Titan Books, 2017
22. Ibid.
23. *Guillermo del Toro – Cabinet of Curiosities: My Notebooks, Collections, and Other Obsessions*, Guillermo del Toro and Marc Scott Zicree, Titan Books, 2013
24. *Show The Monster*, Daniel Zalewski, *The New Yorker*, 31 January 2011
25. *A Conversation with Guillermo del Toro*, Jeff Otto, *IGN*, 31 May 2012
26. Ibid.
27. Ibid.
28. *Monster's Ball*, David Edelstein, *Slate*, 1 April 2004
29. *Guillermo del Toro Interview for The Book of Life: What is it With Mexicans and death?*, Horatia Harrod, *The Telegraph*, 25 October 2014
30. *Guillermo del Toro – Guardian Interviews at the BFI*, Mark Kermode, 21 November 2006
31. Ibid.
32. *Set Visit: Interview with Hellboy II Director Guillermo del Toro*, Jason Adams, *Joblo.com*, 4 February 2008
33. Ibid.
34. Ibid.
35. *How I Made Hellboy in My Image*, Guillermo del Toro, *The Guardian*, 27 July 2008
36. *Guillermo del Toro – Cabinet of Curiosities: My Notebooks, Collections, and Other Obsessions*, Guillermo del Toro and Marc Scott Zicree, Titan Books, 2013
37. *Mike Mignola on Hellboy's future – and Which Character Almost Debuted in Hellboy 2*, Rick Marshall, *mtv.com*, 18 April 2010
38. *Set Visit: Interview with Hellboy II Director Guillermo del Toro*, Jason Adams, *Joblo.com*, 4 February 2008
39. *Monster Mash*, Christopher Orr, *The New Republic*, 27 July 2004

Rites of Passage

1. *Pan's Labyrinth*, Lisa Schwarzbaum, *Entertainment Weekly*, 1 January 2007
2. *In Gloom of War, a Child's Paradise*, A.O. Scott, *The New York Times*, 29 December 2006
3. *Pan's Labyrinth – BFI Film Classics*, Mar Diestro-Dópido, Bloomsbury, 2013
4. *Guillermo del Toro's Pan's Labyrinth*, Nick Nunziata, Mark Cotta Vaz, and Guillermo del Toro, Titan Books, 2016
5. Ibid.
6. *Harry Potter at 20: Guillermo del Toro Regrets Turning Down the Chance to Direct*, Hanna Flint, *Independent*, 26 June 2017
7. *Guillermo del Toro's The Devil's Backbone*, Matt Zoller Seitz & Simon Abrams, Titan Books, 2017
8. *Pan's Labyrinth Blu-ray Edition*, The Criterion Edition, 18 October 2016
9. *Guillermo del Toro Interviewed – Pan's Labyrinth*, Steve 'Frosty' Weintraub, *Collider*, 3 January 2007
10. *Pan's Labyrinth – BFI Film Classics*, Mar Diestro-Dópido, Bloomsbury, 2013
11. Ibid.
12. *Guillermo del Toro's Pan's Labyrinth*, Nick Nunziata, Mark Cotta Vaz, and Guillermo del Toro, Titan Books, 2016
13. *Guillermo del Toro – Guardian Interviews at the BFI*, Mark Kermode, *The Guardian*, 21 November 2006

14. Ibid.
15. *Guillermo del Toro's Pan's Labyrinth*, Nick Nunziata, Mark Cotta Vaz, and Guillermo del Toro, Titan Books, 2016
16. *Guillermo del Toro – Guardian Interviews at the BFI*, Mark Kermode, 21 November 2006
17. *Pan's Labyrinth – BFI Film Classics*, Mar Diestro-Dópido, Bloomsbury, 2013
18. *Guillermo del Toro Interviewed – Pan's Labyrinth*, Steve 'Frosty' Weintraub, *Collider*, 3 January 2007
19. *Guillermo del Toro's Pan's Labyrinth*, Nick Nunziata, Mark Cotta Vaz, and Guillermo del Toro, Titan Books, 2016
20. *Pan's Labyrinth – Interview with Guillermo del Toro*, Michael Guillen, *Screen Anarchy*, 17 December 2006
21. *Pan's Labyrinth Blu-ray Edition*, The Criterion Edition, 18 October 2016
22. *Guillermo del Toro Interviewed – Pan's Labyrinth*, Steve 'Frosty' Weintraub, *Collider*, 3 January 2007
23. *Pan's Labyrinth Blu-ray Edition*, The Criterion Edition, 18 October 2016
24. Ibid.
25. Ibid.
26. Ibid.
27. *Guillermo del Toro – Cabinet of Curiosities: My Notebooks, Collections, and Other Obsessions*, Guillermo del Toro and Marc Scott Zicree, Titan Books, 2013
28. Ibid.
29. *Guillermo del Toro Interviewed – Pan's Labyrinth*, Steve 'Frosty' Weintraub, *Collider*, 3 January 2007
30. *Guillermo del Toro's Pan's Labyrinth*, Nick Nunziata, Mark Cotta Vaz, and Guillermo del Toro, Titan Books, 2016
31. *Pan's Labyrinth Blu-ray Edition*, The Criterion Edition, 18 October 2016
32. *Pan's Labyrinth – BFI Film Classics*, Mar Diestro-Dópido, Bloomsbury, 2013
33. *Show The Monster*, Daniel Zalewski, *The New Yorker*, 31 January 2011
34. *Guillermo del Toro – Cabinet of Curiosities: My Notebooks, Collections, and Other Obsessions*, Guillermo del Toro and Marc Scott Zicree, Titan Books, 2013
35. *Girl Interrupted*, Mark Kermode, *Sight & Sound*, 2 December 2006
36. *Guillermo del Toro's The Devil's Backbone*, Matt Zoller Seitz & Simon Abrams, Titan Books, 2017
37. Ibid.
38. *Guillermo del Toro – Cabinet of Curiosities: My Notebooks, Collections, and Other Obsessions*, Guillermo del Toro and Marc Scott Zicree, Titan Books, 2013
39. *Pan's Labyrinth – Interview with Guillermo del Toro*, Michael Guillen, *Screen Anarchy*, 17 December 2006
40. *Guillermo del Toro – Cabinet of Curiosities: My Notebooks, Collections, and Other Obsessions*, Guillermo del Toro and Marc Scott Zicree, Titan Books, 2013
41. *Pan's Labyrinth – Interview with Guillermo del Toro*, Michael Guillen, *Screen Anarchy*, 17 December 2006
42. *Guillermo del Toro – Cabinet of Curiosities: My Notebooks, Collections, and Other Obsessions*, Guillermo del Toro and Marc Scott Zicree, Titan Books, 2013
43. *Guillermo del Toro Dazzles With The Shape of Water: 'Inspiration is a Mystery for Everyone'*, Dylan Kai Dempsey, *Nofilmschool.com*, 13 September 2017
44. *Guillermo del Toro's Pan's Labyrinth*, Nick Nunziata, Mark Cotta Vaz, and Guillermo del Toro, Titan Books, 2016

45. Ibid.
46. *The Craft of the Director: Guillermo del Toro, Directors Guild of America via YouTube*, 7 May 2018
47. *Guillermo del Toro – Cabinet of Curiosities: My Notebooks, Collections, and Other Obsessions*, Guillermo del Toro and Marc Scott Zicree, Titan Books, 2013
48. Ibid.
49. *Guillermo del Toro's Pan's Labyrinth*, Nick Nunziata, Mark Cotta Vaz, and Guillermo del Toro, Titan Books, 2016
50. Ibid.
51. *Pan's Labyrinth – BFI Film Classics*, Mar Diestro-Dópido, Bloomsbury, 2013
52. *Guillermo del Toro's Pan's Labyrinth*, Nick Nunziata, Mark Cotta Vaz, and Guillermo del Toro, Titan Books, 2016
53. *Pan's Labyrinth – Interview with Guillermo del Toro*, Michael Guillen, *Screen Anarchy*, 17 December 2006

High Concept

1. *Guillermo del Toro – Cabinet of Curiosities: My Notebooks, Collections, and Other Obsessions*, Guillermo del Toro and Marc Scott Zicree, Titan Books, 2013
2. *Guillermo del Toro's The Devil's Backbone*, Matt Zoller Seitz & Simon Abrams, Titan Books, 2017
3. *The Den of Geek Interview: Guillermo del Toro*, Simon Brew, *Den of Geek*, 14 July 2008
4. *Guillermo del Toro – Cabinet of Curiosities: My Notebooks, Collections, and Other Obsessions*, Guillermo del Toro and Marc Scott Zicree, Titan Books, 2013
5. *Guillermo del Toro's Monte Cristo inspired project called The Left Hand of Darkness!*, Harry Knowles, *Aintitcool.com*, 5 July 2002
6. Ibid.
7. Ibid.
8. *The Den of Geek Interview: Guillermo del Toro*, Simon Brew, *Den of Geek*, 14 July 2008
9. *Guillermo del Toro's Frankenstein Monster was 'Hauntingly Beautiful,' Says Doug Jones*, Vinnie Mancuso, *Collider*, 29 October 2020
10. *Show The Monster*, Daniel Zalewski, *The New Yorker*, 31 January 2011
11. Ibid.
12. *The Den of Geek Interview: Guillermo del Toro*, Simon Brew, *Den of Geek*, 14 July 2008
13. *Anything You Can Imagine: Peter Jackson and the Making of Middle-earth*, Ian Nathan, Harper Collins, 2018
14. *Show The Monster*, Daniel Zalewski, *The New Yorker*, 31 January 2011
15. Ibid.
16. Ibid.
17. *Guillermo del Toro Interviewed – Pan's Labyrinth*, Steve 'Frosty' Weintraub, *Collider*, 3 January 2007
18. *Show The Monster*, Daniel Zalewski, *The New Yorker*, 31 January 2011
19. Ibid.
20. *Q&A: Guillermo del Toro On Why He Will Next Direct Pacific Rim After At The Mountains Of Madness Fell Apart*, Mike Fleming Jr., *Deadline*, 9 March 2011
21. *Guillermo del Toro: 'Madness has gone Dark'*, Daniel Zalewski, *The New Yorker*, 8 March 2011
22. *Guillermo del Toro Will Fight to His Grave to Get At t he Mountains of Madness Made*, Neeraj Chand, *Movieweb*, 2 July 2020

23. *Guillermo del Toro Explains What Happened To At The Mountains Of Madness, Pacific Rim Is Next*, Eric Eisenberg, *Cinemaweb*, 9 March 2011
24. *Pacific Rim: Man, Machines & Monsters*, David S. Cohen, Titan Books, 2013
25. *Guillermo del Toro interview: Pacific Rim, Monsters and More*, Ryan Lambie, *Den of Geek*, 12 July 2013
26. Ibid.
27. *Pacific Rim Blu-ray*, Warner Home Video, 11 November 2015
28. *Interview: Guillermo del Toro on the Future of Pacific Rim 2, His Dream to Make a Noir, and Why He Flipped the Gender Script for Crimson Peak*, Carolyn Cox, *The Mary Sue*, 15 October 2015
29. Ibid.
30. *Guillermo del Toro interview: Pacific Rim, Monsters and More*, Ryan Lambie, *Den of Geek*, 12 July 2013
31. Ibid.
32. *Guillermo del Toro Interviewed – Pan's Labyrinth*, Steve 'Frosty' Weintraub, *Collider*, 3 January 2007
33. *Inside Pacific Rim with Guillermo del Toro*, David S. Cohen, *Variety*, 29 May 2013
34. Ibid.
35. *Guillermo del Toro Talks Getting Back in the Director's Chair, the Evolution of the Script, Creating the World on a Giant Scale, and More on the Set of Pacific Rim*, Steve Weintraub, *Collider*, 19 June 2013
36. *Review: Pacific Rim*, Max Nelson, *Film Comment*, 11 July 2013
37. Ibid.
38. *Guillermo del Toro interview: Pacific Rim, Monsters and More*, Ryan Lambie, *Den of Geek*, 12 July 2013
39. *Pacific Rim*, Dana Stevens, *Slate*, 11 July 2013

Sidebar: The Others

1. *Interview: No Mimic; Guillermo del Toro Declares His Independence with Devil's Backbone*, Anthony Kaufman, *IndieWire*, 27 November 2001
2. *Guillermo del Toro Talks Tarzan*, unattributed, *Comicbookmovie.com*, 15 February 2007

Freak House

1. *Guillermo del Toro – Cabinet of Curiosities: My Notebooks, Collections, and Other Obsessions*, Guillermo del Toro and Marc Scott Zicree, Titan Books, 2013
2. *Crimson Peak Blu-ray*, Arrow Video, 2019
3. *The Guillermo del Toro Haunted Mansion Remake We Never Got To See*, Eric Betts, *Looper.com*, 25 September 2020
4. Ibid.
5. Ibid.
6. Ibid.
7. *Crimson Peak Blu-ray*, Arrow Video, 2019
8. *Guillermo del Toro Describes his Real-life Encounter with a Ghost*, Meredith Woerner, *Gizmodo*, 25 January 2013
9. Ibid.
10. *At the Mountains of Madness*, H.P. Lovecraft, 1931
11. *Exclusive: Crimson Peak 'Shockingly Different' for del Toro, Guillermo On Kinky Nature of Gothic Tale*, Ryan Turek, *Comingsoon.net*, 30 June 2013

12. *Interview: Guillermo del Toro on the Future of Pacific Rim 2, His Dream to Make a Noir, and Why He Flipped the Gender Script for Crimson Peak*, Carolyn Cox, *The Mary Sue*, 15 October 2015
13. Ibid.
14. *Gothic: The Dark Heart of Film*, BFI, 2013
15. Ibid.
16. *Guillermo del Toro on England giving him the creeps and setting Crimson Peak in the UK*, Tom Huddleston, *Time Out*, 13 October 2015
17. *The New Biographical Dictionary of Film*, David Thomson, Little Brown, 2002
18. *Exclusive: Crimson Peak 'Shockingly Different' for del Toro, Guillermo On Kinky Nature of Gothic Tale*, Ryan Turek, *Comingsoon.net*, 30 June 2013
19. *Crimson Peak: New Poster of the Guillermo del Toro Horror*, David Crow, *Den of Geek*, 5 August 2015
20. *'Guillermo's Got a Wonderfully Unhealthy Obsession with Insects': Screenwriter Matthew Robbins on Crimson Peak*, Matt Mulcahey, *Filmmaker*, 26 October 2015
21. *Guillermo del Toro Talks Crimson Peak, Pacific Rim 2*, Brendon Connelly, *Den of Geek*, 13 October 2015
22. Ibid.
23. *Gothic: The Dark Heart of Film*, BFI, 2013
24. Ibid.
25. *Interview: Guillermo del Toro on the Future of Pacific Rim 2, His Dream to Make a Noir, and Why He Flipped the Gender Script for Crimson Peak*, Carolyn Cox, *The Mary Sue*, 15 October 2015
26. *Guillermo del Toro Talks Crimson Peak, Building a Massive 3-Story House, Crafting a 'Kinky and Violent' Gothic Romance, Creating Ghosts, and More on Set*, Steve Weintraub, *Collider*, 17 July 2014
27. *Guillermo del Toro To Direct Crimson Peak; Could Mountains of Madness Happen?*, Sandy Schaeffer, *Screen Rant*, 4 December 2012
28. *Gothic: The Dark Heart of Film*, BFI, 2013
29. *Guillermo del Toro on Serenading Crews, Silent Hills and Crimson Peak*, Brad Miska, *Bloody Disgusting*, 7 October 2015
30. *Crimson Peak Blu-ray*, Arrow Video, 2019
31. *Guillermo del Toro on England giving him the creeps and setting Crimson Peak in the UK*, Tom Huddleston, *Time Out*, 13 October 2015
32. *Crimson Peak: a Gothic romance to Die For*, David Sims, *The Atlantic*, 16 October 2015
33. *Review: Crimson Peak*, Violet Lucca, *Film Comment*, 21 October 2015
34. *She's Leaving Home*, Stuart Klawans, *The Nation*, 5 November 2015

The Love Aquatic

1. *Guillermo del Toro Wins Best Director Award for Shape of Water at Oscars 2018*, Andrew Pulver, *The Guardian*, 5 March 2018
2. *Guillermo del Toro on his Oscar Wins and How to Push for Inclusion in Hollywood*, Kristopher Tapley, *Variety*, 7 March 2018
3. *How Guillermo del Toro's Black Lagoon Fantasy Inspired Shape of Water*, Borys Kit, *The Hollywood Reporter*, 3 November 2017
4. *Guillermo del Toro Talks Frankenstein and The Creature from the Black Lagoon*, Joey Paur, *Greek Tyrant*, 2014

5. Ibid.
6. Ibid.
7. *Guillermo del Toro on The Shape of Water, the Beauty of Monsters, and Connecting with Lady Bird*, Christina Radish, *Collider*, 12 February 2018
8. Ibid.
9. *How Guillermo del Toro's Black Lagoon Fantasy Inspired Shape of Water*, Borys Kit, *The Hollywood Reporter*, 3 November 2017
10. Ibid.
11. Ibid.
12. *The Shape of Water with Guillermo del Toro, The New York Times Talks* via YouTube, 28 November 2017
13. *Beauty and the Beasts*, Rob Field, *DGA.org*, Winter 2014
14. Ibid.
15. *The Shape of Water: Creating a Fairy Tale for Troubled Times*, Gina McIntyre, Titan Books, 2017
16. *The Genre-Fluid Fantasy of the Shape of Water*, Anthony Lane, *The New Yorker*, 11 December 2017
17. Ibid.
18. *Guillermo del Toro's The Devil's Backbone*, Matt Zoller Seitz & Simon Abrams, Titan Books, 2017
19. *Guillermo del Toro on The Shape of Water, the Beauty of Monsters, and Connecting with Lady Bird*, Christina Radish, *Collider*, 12 February 2018
20. Ibid.
21. *The Shape of Water: Creating a Fairy Tale for Troubled Times*, Gina McIntyre, Titan Books, 2017
22. Ibid.
23. Ibid.
24. The Shape of Water with Guillermo del Toro, *The New York Times Talks* via YouTube, 28 November 2017
25. Ibid.
26. Ibid.
27. *Guillermo del Toro – Cabinet of Curiosities: My Notebooks, Collections, and Other Obsessions*, Guillermo del Toro and Marc Scott Zicree, Titan Books, 2013
28. *Like his Blue-collar Demon Hero Hellboy, Guillermo del Toro has a Few Issues with Authority*, unattributed, *The Scotsman*, 15 August 2008
29. *The Shape of Water: Creating a Fairy Tale for Troubled Times*, Gina McIntyre, Titan Books, 2017
30. Ibid.
31. *The Shape of Water Blu-ray*, 20th Century Fox, 2018
32. *The Shape of Water: Guillermo del Toro Defends the Full-Frontal Nudity of his Oscar-nominated Film*, Tom Butler, *Yahoo Movies*, 14 February 2018
33. *The Shape of Water with Guillermo del Toro, The New York Times Talks* via YouTube, 28 November 2017

The Weaver of Dreams

1. *Nightmare Alley*, William Lindsay Gresham, The New York Review of Books, 1976 edition
2. *Guillermo del Toro: The interview, Part II*, Ethan Gilsdorf, *Wired*, 23 August 2011
3. *Interview: Guillermo del Toro on the Future of Pacific Rim 2, His Dream to Make a Noir, and Why He Flipped the Gender Script for Crimson Peak*, Carolyn Cox, *The Mary Sue*, 15 October 2015
4. *Guillermo del Toro Talks Scary Stories, Nightmare Alley, and Bringing His Fantasies to Life*, Andrew Barker, *Variety*, 6 August 2019

5. *Guillermo del Toro Talks Nightmare Alley and Pinocchio*, Gary Collinson, *Flickering Myth*, 15 August 2019

6. Ibid.

7. *Tarot del Toro*, Guillermo del Toro & Tomas Hijo, Insight Editions, 2020

8. Ibid.

9. Ibid.

10. Ibid.

11. *Nightmare Alley*, William Lindsay Gresham, The New York Review of Books, 1976 edition

12. *Righting a Wrong*, Guillermo del Toro, *Twitter*, 9 October 2015

13. *Guillermo del Toro's Nightmare Alley Wraps Production with Cooper, Blanchett, Mara, and More*, Ryan Lattanzio, *IndieWire*, 12 December 2020

14. *Exclusive: Guillermo del Toro on Netflix, Roma, and Why He's Making Pinocchio*, Helen Barlow, *Collider*, 21 December 2018

15. *'Guillermo's Got a Wonderfully Unhealthy Obsession with Insects': Screenwriter Matthew Robbins on Crimson Peak*, Matt Mulcahey, *Filmmaker*, 26 October 2015

16. *Guillermo del Toro's Pinocchio 'As Far as You Can Get From the Disney-fied Version' Says One of Film's Writers*, Josh Weiss, *SyFy Wire*, 14 January 2021

17. *Guillermo del Toro – Cabinet of Curiosities: My Notebooks, Collections, and Other Obsessions*, Guillermo del Toro and Marc Scott Zicree, Titan Books, 2013

18. *Guillermo del Toro Working on Darker Version of Pinocchio*, Sandy Schaeffer, *Screen Rant*, 17 February 2011

19. Ibid.

20. *Guillermo del Toro's Pinocchio 'As Far as You Can Get From the Disney-fied Version' Says One of Film's Writers*, Josh Weiss, *SyFy Wire*, 14 January 2021

21. *Exclusive: Guillermo del Toro on Netflix, Roma, and Why He's Making Pinocchio*, Helen Barlow, *Collider*, 21 December 2018

22. *Marrakech: Guillermo del Toro Talks "Political" 'Pinocchio,' Confirms 'Terrified' Remake*, Rhonda Richford, *The Hollywood Reporter*, 1 December 2018

23. *Exclusive: Guillermo del Toro on Netflix, Roma, and Why He's Making Pinocchio*, Helen Barlow, *Collider*, 21 December 2018

24. *Guillermo del Toro's The Devil's Backbone*, Matt Zoller Seitz & Simon Abrams, Titan Books, 2017

25. *Guillermo del Toro Talks Scary Stories, Nightmare Alley, and Bringing His Fantasies to Life*, Andrew Barker, *Variety*, 6 August 2019

Acknowledgements

As this series gains further ground, it goes without saying that the foremost source of inspiration, pleasure, terror, (intended) revulsion, thrill, and feast for thought is the great man himself – Guillermo del Toro. What a towering subject: not only for the films, but for his account of those films, revealing vast and hidden depths. I have been happily lost in that labyrinth for months. It might be, I will never return. So my unreserved thanks go the maestro – *Nunca dejes que se aleje la luz*. I can only hope this volume contributes to the libraries of appreciation that will surely be written. My thanks also go to my editor Jessica Axe at Quarto, for encouraging words and firm leadership; to Joe Hallsworth, given the unenviable task of suggesting there might be a deadline; to copy-editor Nick Freeth, who has shouldered the added burden of nailing every accent to every Latin spelling; and Sue Pressley at Stonecastle Graphics, who has once again delivered the eye protein. I will always remember those that have advised and helped in subtle ways. And finally my love and endless gratitude go to Kat, who has never trusted fairies.

PICTURE CREDITS

AA Film Archive / Alamy Stock Photo 09, 41, 91; AF archive / Alamy Stock Photo 08, 23, 55, 150, 156-157r, 158, 103; Album / Alamy Stock Photo 48b, 53b, 61a, 61b, 62, 68b, 85, 94, 102, 107, 154, 159a, 169; Sydney Alford / Alamy Stock Photo 166l; Allstar Picture Library Ltd. / Alamy Stock Photo 100, 136-137; Atlaspix / Alamy Stock Photo 66; BFA / Alamy Stock Photo 57, 98, 113; Matteo Chinellato / Alamy Stock Photo 170c; Collection Christophel / Alamy Stock Photo 22, 51b, 67b, 80bl, 99, 156a; Matthew Corrigan / Alamy Stock Photo 68a; EFE News Agency / Alamy Stock Photo 68a; Entertainment Pictures / Alamy Stock Photo 73, 82a, 82b, 88a, 101b, 108, 109; Everett Collection Inc / Alamy Stock Photo 16, 30, 44, 53a, 56, 67a, 86, 87, 88-89r, 162-163, 164; Raymond Fujioka 70, 72; Granger Historical Picture Archive / Alamy Stock Photo 129, 134; Chris Hellier / Alamy Stock Photo 168; Kathy Hutchins / Alamy Stock Photo 171; Moviestore Collection Ltd / Alamy Stock Photo 15, 25a, 25b, 32, 93, 97, 105; MRP / Alamy Stock Photo 170l; PA Images / Alamy Stock Photo 160; Doug Peters / Alamy Stock Photo 170r; Photo 12 / Alamy Stock Photo 11, 12r, 18, 37, 39b, 42, 81, 84, 92, 96, 104, 106, 141; Pictorial Press Ltd / Alamy Stock Photo 116l; PictureLux / The Hollywood Archive / Alamy Stock Photo 19, 73, 88b, 95, 165; propstore.com 28; The Protected Art Archive / Alamy Stock Photo 116r; Public Domain 112l; Retro AdArchives / Alamy Stock Photo 12l, 59l, 59r, 112r; REUTERS / Alamy Stock Photo 06-07, 24, 58; ScreenProd / Photononstop / Alamy Stock Photo 36; Sueddeutsche Zeitung Photo / Alamy Stock Photo 13; TCD/Prod.DB / Alamy Stock Photo 4-5, 17, 20, 21, 27, 31, 33r, 34, 35, 39a, 43, 45, 46, 47, 48a, 49, 50, 51a, 52, 54, 63a, 63b, 64-65, 74, 75, 76-77, 77r, 78, 80ar, 83, 110-111, 114-115, 117, 118-119, 120, 121, 122, 123a, 123b, 124-125, 126a, 126b, 127, 128, 130-131, 132, 133, 135, 138, 139, 140, 142, 143a, 143b, 144, 145, 147, 148, 149, 151, 152, 153, 155-156r, 156b159b, 161, 166r, 167; United Archives GmbH / Alamy Stock Photo 38, 60; Universal Pictures / Album / Alamy Stock Photo 146; UPI / Alamy Stock Photo 90; Joshua White / JWPictures.com 69, 71; Wikimedia Creative Commons 10, 26, 29; World History Archive / Alamy Stock Photo 14, 101a; ZUMA Press, Inc. / Alamy Stock Photo 40.

GATEFOLD

Cronos: TCD/Prod.DB / Alamy Stock Photo; *Mimic:* Everett Collection, Inc. / Alamy Stock Photo; *The Devil's Backbone:* AF archive / Alamy Stock Photo; *Blade II:* BFA / Alamy Stock Photo; *Hellboy:* Photo 12 / Alamy Stock Photo; *Pan's Labyrinth:* BFA / Alamy Stock Photo; *The Orphanage:* Everett Collection, Inc. / Alamy Stock Photo; *Hellboy II:* Everett Collection, Inc. / Alamy Stock Photo; *Splice:* Everett Collection Inc / Alamy Stock Photo; *Don't be Afraid of the Dark:* TCD/Prod.DB / Alamy Stock Photo; *Pacific Rim:* TCD/Prod.DB / Alamy Stock Photo; *Mama:* Album / Alamy Stock Photo; *Live. Die. Repeat.:* Collection Christophel / Alamy Stock; Photo; *The Hobbit:* AF archive / Alamy Stock Photo; *The Strain:* Album / Alamy Stock Photo; *Crimson Peak:* Photo 12 / Alamy Stock Photo; *The Shape of Water:* TCD/Prod. DB / Alamy Stock Photo; *Scary Stories:* Album / Alamy Stock Photo; *The Witches:* BFA / Alamy Stock Photo; *Antlers:* Fox Searchlight Pictures.